LARK JEWELRY & BEADING
beadweaving master class

MAGGIE MEISTER'S
CLASSICAL ELEGANCE

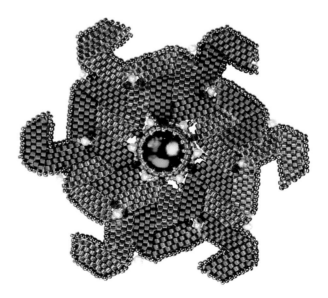

LARK JEWELRY & BEADING
beadweaving master class

MAGGIE MEISTER'S
CLASSICAL ELEGANCE
20 BEADED JEWELRY DESIGNS

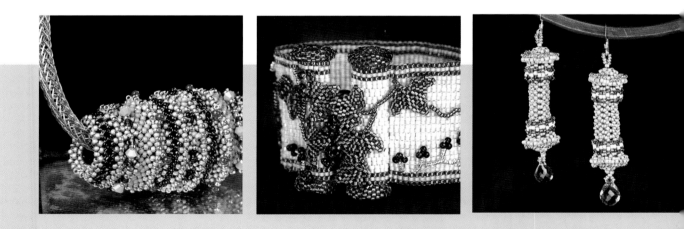

LARK
CRAFTS

An Imprint of Sterling Publishing Co., Inc.
New York

WWW.LARKCRAFTS.COM

Senior Editor
Ray Hemachandra

Editor
Nathalie Mornu

Technical Editor
Judith Durant

Art Director
Kathy Holmes

Junior Designer
Carol Morse Barnao

Art Production
Celia Naranjo

Illustrators
J'aime Allene
Bonnie Brooks

Photographer
Stewart O'Shields

Cover Designer
Celia Naranjo

Editorial Assistance
Abby Haffelt

Library of Congress Cataloging-in-Publication Data

Meister, Maggie.
 [Classical elegance]
 Maggie Meister's classical elegance : 20 beaded jewelry designs. -- 1st ed.
    p. cm.
 Includes bibliographical references and index.
 ISBN 978-1-60059-691-9 (hc-plc : alk. paper)
 1. Jewelry making. 2. Bead work. I. Title.
 TT212.M44 2011
 739.27--dc22

                          2010045131

10 9 8 7 6 5 4 3 2 1

First Edition

Published by Lark Crafts
An Imprint of Sterling Publishing Co., Inc.
387 Park Avenue South, New York, NY 10016

Text © 2011, Maggie Meister
Photography © 2011, Lark Crafts, an Imprint of Sterling Publishing Co., Inc., unless otherwise specified
Illustrations © 2011, Lark Crafts, an Imprint of Sterling Publishing Co., Inc., unless otherwise specified

Distributed in Canada by Sterling Publishing,
c/o Canadian Manda Group, 165 Dufferin Street
Toronto, Ontario, Canada M6K 3H6

Distributed in the United Kingdom by GMC Distribution Services,
Castle Place, 166 High Street, Lewes, East Sussex, England BN7 1XU

Distributed in Australia by Capricorn Link (Australia) Pty Ltd.,
P.O. Box 704, Windsor, NSW 2756 Australia

If you have questions or comments about this book, please contact:
Lark Crafts
67 Broadway
Asheville, NC 28801
828-253-0467

Manufactured in China

All rights reserved

ISBN 13: 978-1-60059-691-9

For information about custom editions, special sales, and premium and corporate purchases, please contact the Sterling Special Sales Department at 800-805-5489 or specialsales@sterlingpub.com.

For information about desk and examination copies available to college and university professors, submit requests to academic@larkbooks.com. Our complete policy can be found at www.larkcrafts.com.

CONTENTS

INTRODUCTION

BEADS AND ANTIQUITY ARE MY TWO GREAT LOVES.

As far back as I can remember, I've enjoyed exploring both history and jewelry—whether it was sitting in my father's den perusing his books on Pompeii and Roman history or adorning myself with the Czechoslovakian-glass Mardi Gras beads that my aunt sent me every year. These passions merged when I was fortunate enough to live in Italy for five years.

I discovered seed beads prior to moving there and had taken many workshops while employed at a bead shop. I was familiar with various beadweaving stitches and even played with combining stitches after a workshop with Carol Wilcox Wells. It wasn't until the splendors of Naples surrounded me that I found my source of inspiration, and seed beads became a medium for me to capture the memory of what I saw.

By beading components and combining stitches, I can build and interpret the patterns and motifs I come across. I can create the three-dimensional curves found in a mosaic, for instance, or the lines and shapes from a rug pattern.

This book begins with a section that explains the various stitches I use in the projects. I also include directions for combining stitches. Once you become proficient in the basic stitches, the projects build on the knowledge. The best way to use this book is to familiarize yourself with the basic stitches and practice, practice, practice!

Run through the basics of circular peyote, for example. After some practice, you can make the Rosette earrings (page 114), which use a variation of circular peyote and embellishment to make simple but elegant baubles. In the same vein, review and do a trial run of brick stitch, and learn how to bezel a coin pearl with circular peyote. Apply a bezel to a few more pearls, until you really get it. After that, you're ready to go to the Tuccia earrings project (page 81), where you'll find out how to follow a pattern made with brick stitch and how to increase on the ends. These earrings feature bezeled coin pearls, and by this time you will likely be a bezeling pro.

I've organized the 20 projects based on what influenced my designs. One chapter contains pieces inspired by historical jewelry. For example, the Matriarchs' Cuff on page 30 builds on a Jewish wedding ring from the seventeenth century. In another chapter, mosaics and textile patterns guide the aesthetics of the projects, as seen in the Sappho Necklace (page 84), which incorporates two mosaic designs in its lyre shapes and herringbone borders. For the final chapter, I gleaned ideas from the great buildings and various architectural elements I've seen. I borrowed the shape of the onion-dome church steeples found throughout Europe for the Santa Sofia Pendant (page 98), and the frescoes in the ancient Villa Oplonti served as a model for the Oplonti bracelet on page 110.

You'll see that many of my designs consist of smaller components joined together. These constituent parts are very versatile. The Artemisia earrings (page 104), for instance, consist of two components, but you could easily bead five and turn them into a bracelet. I'll remind you of this sort of variation wherever appropriate.

I hope this book helps you find your own muse and discover your passions, inspiring you to interpret them with lovely little beads.

Maggie Meister

CHAPTER ONE

BASIC MATERIALS & TOOLS

Beads

Where do I begin? Beads come in so many sizes, shapes, and finishes, it's often hard to decide what to use. Here's what I tend to work with.

Seed Beads

Seed beads come in many sizes and shapes and are manufactured mainly in Europe and Japan. I lean toward Japanese beads because of their uniformity of shape and color.

Cylinder Beads

These beads are like little tesserae (tiles); building blocks that can be used to create sculptural pieces. They're most commonly known by the manufacturers' brand names, Delicas and Aikos (produced by Miyuki and Toho, respectively). My favorites are size 11° cylinder beads, and I'm particularly drawn to the matte metallic and metallic finishes. Many of my projects use beads plated in 24-karat gold or sterling silver, but you could substitute bronze or gray beads.

Size 15° cylinder beads nicely downsize any project that uses size 11° cylinder beads, but because their walls are very thin, I always use a size 12 or 13 needle and single thread.

Round Beads

Size 11° and size 15° round seed beads combine nicely with cylinder beads to give a piece of jewelry more texture and depth. Size 13° and size 15° charlottes, which have one facet or cut, add a little extra shimmer.

Other Beads

Seed beads are the basis of all the projects you'll find in this book, but additional accent beads are essential to almost every piece.

Pearls

Pearls—I just love them! Their reflective finish picks up the colors of the seed beads and adds a wonderful element to any design. Freshwater pearls come in many different shapes and sizes, and my favorites are coin pearls, small seed pearls, and baroque drops. I also like to bezel button pearls, which have a horizontal hole. When you're shopping, pay particular attention to the finish—if you see chips or the finish is dull, stay away.

Glass Beads

Czech fire-polished beads come in great colors and can be a nice substitute for stones and pearls. I'm particularly attracted to "pinch" beads, which are triangular in shape because they add nice texture to a design.

Semiprecious Beads

I use semiprecious and precious stones for embellishing designs because they can make a piece look ancient. It's important to buy the best quality stones you can afford. I look for depth of color and quality of cut. Check around the edge of the holes to see if they're chipped or cut—reject them if they are because they'll cut your thread. My favorite stones are garnets, lapis, turquoise, rubies, and emeralds, and I use mostly 2- and 3-mm beads.

Crystals

Although I don't use a lot of crystals in my work, I'm still drawn to them. Of the millions of styles available, I primarily use 2-mm and 3-mm Swarovski rounds because they add just enough sparkle and remind me of small stones. I also like the Swarovski drops, which can be substituted for a pearl or semiprecious drop.

Thread

Ah, the Great Thread Wars! Everyone has her or his own preference—and opinion—for thread, and I firmly believe that you should use the thread that you prefer. That said, I think some threads work better than others for particular projects. For example, with crystals it's better to use a braided beading thread (fishing line) such

as Fireline or Wildfire because the crystals won't cut this cord as easily as they will other threads. I don't use braided thread when bezeling a round bead because it doesn't have the give that other threads do, and it often breaks the beads.

Nymo D

This is my favorite. Nymo is a strong twisted nylon thread that was originally used in the shoe and upholstery industries. There's quite a nice selection of colors, and it comes in a variety of sizes from O (thin) to F (thickest), with B and D being the most popular. I primarily use D. It does have a tendency to knot and shred, so I wax it with a microcrystalline wax and use shorter lengths (less than a wingspan—see below if you're unfamiliar with this term) to prevent this problem.

One-G

One-G is manufactured by Toho and is my next choice after Nymo. It's as strong as Nymo but you don't have as extensive a color selection. One-G is available in only one size, much like Nymo D.

LENGTH OF THREAD

I use a little less than a wing-span of thread to keep it from fraying and tangling. A wingspan is equivalent to the distance from one outstretched hand to the other.

SINGLE VERSUS DOUBLED THREAD

The project determines whether I use single or doubled thread. When working in right angle weave, I use single thread because of the many passes through the beads. I also use single thread with brick stitch because doubled thread tends to show between the beads. I double the thread when building three-dimensional components that need to be strong.

Braided Beading Threads

Most of these threads were originally made for the fishing industry. They're pre-waxed, braided, and extremely strong. They come in several different sizes; 4 lb test and 6 lb test are my favorites.

Other threads popular among beaders, such as C-Lon, Silamide, and K-O thread, I very rarely use. I find K-O thread isn't as strong as the others—I can break it right off the spool with my hands. Give them all a try and find your favorite.

Thread Conditioners

Thread treatments make threads more manageable, and I use them on all types of thread.

Microcrystalline Wax

This synthetic wax keeps thread from tangling by conditioning it. It's particularly helpful when you double the thread, because it makes the thread stiffer. I prefer it to beeswax, which can be very sticky.

Thread Heaven

This thread conditioner and protector is made from a synthetic chemical compound. I use both Thread Heaven and microcrystalline wax together. First I pass the needle through the Thread Heaven to prolong the life of the thread, and then through the microcrystalline to stiffen it.

Findings

You'll need a few basic findings for some of the projects. Here's a brief description of what I've used.

Clasps

The clasp is an important part of a piece, and I let the design determine whether I make a beaded closure or use a purchased clasp. If I decide to use a metal clasp, I use sterling silver, gold-filled, or 14-karat gold whenever possible. I like tubular spacer bar clasps for bracelets because it's easy to attach wide pieces of beadwork to the rings on the tube.

Ear Wires & Posts

Earrings are my favorite pieces of jewelry and I use a variety of styles of ear wires in sterling silver, gold-filled, or 14-karat gold. I like the simple French hook design with either a small bead or a twisted wire at the base of the piece. Lever backs are also very elegant and the closed back makes it a secure finding. Finally, the 10-mm pad with a post is great because I can use circular peyote to capture the pad, making it part of the design.

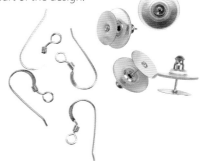

Blanks

I used a brass blank for the Matriarchs' Cuff (page 31). The blank has a square indent in the center and the sides taper at the ends to a soft curve.

Tools

Here's more information about the items I always keep on hand.

Needles

There are many needle manufacturers. I prefer English beading needles because they're slightly thinner and don't break as easily as others.

Beading Needles

Beading needles come in a variety of sizes from 15 (thinnest) to 10 (thickest). I've even seen size 16 needles, but they're hard to come by. (I've often wished I had a size 16 when working with size 22° vintage beads!) I generally use size 10 beading needles with size 11° cylinder and round seed beads. I also use sizes 12 and 13 when working with smaller beads and semiprecious stones because it's easier to pass a thinner needle through the holes.

Sharps

These needles are shorter than beading needles, and although I don't like beading with them all the time, I love to use them when joining components or for getting into tight spaces because they don't break as easily as beading needles do.

Pliers

I always carry flat-nose pliers with me and use them to grab a needle that's stuck in a bead. Simply grasp the tip of a stuck needle and *gently* pull. I like to use the small version of these pliers.

Beading Surface

The velour bead mats sold at your local bead store are the most popular beading surface. They keep the beads from roaming. My favorite beading mat comes in a plastic case 11½ x 15 x 1 inches (29.2 x 38.1 x 2.5 cm). It has velour mats on both sides of the case and it snaps shut to hold a project in place.

Scissors

I use high-quality embroidery scissors to cut threads such as Nymo and One-G, and cheaper scissors for cutting braided beading threads, which will quickly dull the edges of the scissors.

Scoops

I use scoops to pick up little seed beads on the beading surface, and there are several styles on the market. My favorite is the metal triangle; it's easier to pick up beads with a metal edge than a plastic one. The points on the triangle are very sharp, so I often use a point to sort beads that have gone astray.

Task Lamp

My task lamp is as important as my beads. Nothing is more frustrating than not having good light when working! I use a portable full-spectrum task lamp both at home and on the road.

Press'n Seal

Some hollow beaded components need an armature or stuffing so they don't collapse. A few of the projects in this book have such components, which I stuff with Press'n Seal. It's designed as a plastic wrap but it also has some adhesive qualities that help in shaping components. I tear or cut small pieces, roll them into balls, and place them inside the components.

Storage Box

When I'm designing a project, more often than not the first few pieces are not exactly what I was looking for in terms of color or shape. I have a box (or two) that I store these pieces in. I visit this box periodically and often find new designs or components for a different project— what doesn't work for one often works for another.

Basic Beading Kit

In addition to the project-specific materials listed with each design, there are some things you should keep on hand for all of your beading projects. These are components of the Basic Beading Kit that appears at the head of the supply list for each project.

Size 10, 12, and 13 beading needles

Sharps needles

Thread in a variety of colors

Scissors

Thread conditioner

Beading surface

Scoops

Pliers

Good lighting

CHAPTER TWO

THE STITCHES

Most of the projects in this book are intended for the intermediate beader, and this chapter is offered as a reference or refresher. If you need more in-depth information, many wonderful books exist that have more detailed instructions for specific techniques such as right angle weave and peyote stitch.

You'll see red stars in the figures throughout the book; these represent the starting points for steps.

Circular peyote stitch

figure 1

Peyote Stitch

Peyote is an ancient stitch that has been found in many cultures, from ancient Egypt to Native American beadwork. It's an extremely versatile stitch and is perhaps the most popular of all the beadweaving techniques. It can be worked in even-count and odd-count number of beads, and in a circular, flat, or tubular form.

STOPPER BEAD

Before beginning peyote stitch, St. Petersburg chain, and Nepal chain, pick up one bead (of a different color from the beads in the project) and pass the needle through it again so it stays in place on the thread. This is known as a "stopper bead," and it holds the beads on the thread temporarily until they've been passed through again in the work. It's not included in the bead count and you can remove it as soon as the beads are secured.

Flat Even-Count Peyote Stitch

String an even number of beads (eight are shown in the example). Pick up a bead, skip a bead, and pass through the next bead. Continue for the entire row (figure 1).

The beads are now in "up" and "down" positions. To begin the next row, pick up a bead, turn, and pass through the first up

bead. Complete the row by placing one bead between the up beads in the row (figure 2).

Tubular Peyote Stitch

The easiest way to make a tube of peyote stitch is to make a flat piece of even-count peyote as described above and add an extra row on one end of the piece. Fold the piece to form a tube and weave through the up beads of each end to "zip" it closed (figure 3).

Flat Odd-Count Peyote

Odd-count peyote is executed in the same manner as even-count except for the turn on one side of the piece.

String an odd number of beads (seven are shown in the example) and begin as for even-count peyote stitch. When you reach the end of the row, pick up a bead and pass through the bead directly above it. The thread path is similar to a figure eight (figure 4). Complete the next row as for even-count peyote (figure 5).

Two-Drop Peyote

Follow the instructions for flat even- and odd-count peyote (page 13), but use two beads instead of one.

Counting Rows in Peyote Stitch

Rows in peyote are counted on the diagonal or in a zigzag pattern (figure 6).

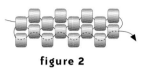

figure 2

figure 3

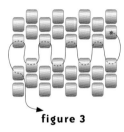

figure 4

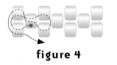

figure 5

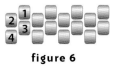

figure 6

13

Increasing and Decreasing in Peyote Stitch

With the thread exiting an up bead, increase by picking up two beads—not one—and pass through the next up bead in the row (figure 7). In the next row, the two beads can either be worked individually with a bead placed between, or the needle can pass through both beads, treating them as one.

With the thread in position to add a bead (bead 1 in figure 8), *decrease* by passing directly through the next up bead without adding a bead. This pulls the piece in.

Stitch in the Ditch with Peyote

A common technique used for embellishment and building with peyote stitch is called stitching in the ditch. With the thread exiting a bead in the row to be embellished, pick up a bead and pass through the next bead in the row (figure 9).

Circular Peyote Stitch

I love this stitch! Once you get the hang of it, the possibilities are endless. If you're not familiar with circular peyote stitch, practice by alternating colors on every other row. The stitch has a series of gradual increases in rows 3 through 6, which form a flat circle. In even-count circular peyote stitch, a "step up" is necessary at the end of each row to get into position to begin the next row. To step up at the end of a row, add the last bead as usual, passing through the last bead of the previous row, then pass through the first bead added in the current row.

Row 1 Pick up three beads and pass through the beads again to form a circle. Step up at the end of the row by passing through the first bead again.

Row 2 *Pick up one bead and pass through the next bead in row 1. Repeat from * two more times, then step up through the first bead added.

Row 3 Here's where the increase begins. *Pick up two beads and pass through the next bead in row 2. Repeat from * two more times to complete the row, adding a total of six beads. At the end of the row, step up through the first bead added, splitting the pair (figure 10).

Row 4 Here's the second step of the gradual increase. With the thread exiting the first bead in a pair, *pick up one bead and pass through the second bead of the pair. Pick up one bead and pass through the first bead of the next pair added in row 3. Repeat from * for the entire row, adding a total of six beads. At the end of the row, step up through the first bead added in this row (figure 11).

Row 5 Work as for row 3, adding a total of 12 beads. At the end of the row, step up through the first bead added, splitting the pair.

Row 6 Work as for row 4, adding a total of 12 beads (figure 12).

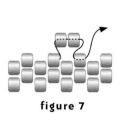

figure 7

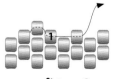

figure 8

figure 9

figure 10

figure 11

figure 12

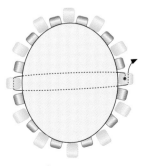

figure 13

Bezeling a Coin Pearl with Peyote Stitch

The instructions below are for bezeling a 10-mm coin pearl with size 11° cylinder beads, but it can be adjusted to fit a 12- or an 8-mm coin or button-style pearl. I often bezel pearls using my favorite colors, to no specific end, and keep them at the ready for use in future projects. They also make great earrings, closures, or bracelets when joined together.

1 Complete rows 1 through 6 of circular peyote stitch (page 14).

2 With the thread exiting an up bead in row 6, position the pearl on top of the flat circular piece of beadwork. Pass through the hole in the pearl and into the sixth up bead—this is the bead that is directly across from the bead that was originally exited. I call this a figure-eight anchor.

3 Pass back through the pearl and into the opposite end of the starting bead as shown (figure 13). Repeat to strengthen the hold.

4 Continue with rows of regular peyote stitch until the sides of the pearl are covered and the pearl is captured in the beadwork. I often work a final row with size 15° round seed beads to both pull the beads in over the pearl *and* add embellishment.

To bezel a 12-mm or larger pearl, increase in row 8 with two beads in every other spot. Treat these two beads as one when stitching subsequent rows.

To bezel a smaller button-style pearl (with a flat bottom and a horizontal hole), anchor the pearl using the figure-eight technique mentioned in step 2 after row 4 is completed and follow the instructions above. The most important thing is to encapsulate the pearl and cover the edges without letting thread show. Add more rows if they're needed; if it's not necessary to increase by adding two beads in one spot, don't do it.

Ladder Stitch

A bead ladder can be used as the base row for brick stitch and herringbone stitch, but I often also use this simple stitch to join components.

1 Pick up two beads and pass through them again (figure 14).

2 Adjust the beads so they sit side by side with the holes facing up and down. With the thread exiting the bottom of the second bead, pick up one bead and pass down through the second bead again, then pass up through the bead just added (figure 15).

Follow the thread path in step 2 to join different components or to form a strip into a circle.

Brick Stitch

This is the first stitch I learned and it's still one of my favorites. The beads sit between the beads in the previous row and resemble bricks in a wall. Brick stitch lends itself perfectly to patterns and it's also a very strong stitch, which makes it perfect for building components.

There are a few different ways to work the first row in brick stitch, but my favorite is to make a bead ladder.

Row 1 (bead ladder) Following the instructions for ladder stitch, make a bead ladder of the desired number of beads (six are used in the example).
Tip: To avoid loose tension of the base ladder row, tighten it up by weaving back through the beads to the beginning of the row.

Row 2 Pick up two beads, pass under the second connecting thread (shown in red), and up through the second bead (figure 16).
Note: Always, always begin each row of brick stitch (in any form) with two beads. This is done so the thread won't show on the edge of the first bead.

*Pick up one bead, pass under the next connecting thread, and back up through the added bead (figure 17). Repeat from * to finish the row. Flip the piece to work from left to right on each row. Note that the piece naturally decreases to a point.

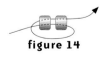

figure 14

figure 15

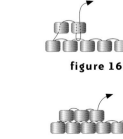

figure 16

figure 17

figure 18

figure 19

figure 20

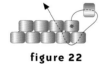

figure 21

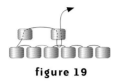

figure 22

figure 23

figure 24

Increasing and Decreasing with Brick Stitch

To increase in brick stitch, add two beads into the same connecting thread, one bead at a time, as shown in figure 18; the beads numbered 2 and 3 share the same connecting thread.

To decrease in brick stitch, pick up one bead, skip the next connecting thread, and pass under the connecting thread that follows (figure 19).

Tubular Brick Stitch

Row 1 Make a bead ladder with the requisite number of beads. Join the first bead to the last bead (figure 20).

Row 2 Continue with brick stitch as previously shown for each row. At the end of a row, add the last bead using the last connecting thread, then join it to the first bead as was done in row 1.

Diagonal Brick Stitch

Working brick stitch on the diagonal is the same as basic flat brick stitch but with increasing and decreasing at the beginning or end of the row.

1 Make a ladder with an odd number of beads (five are used in the example).

2 Pick up two beads and pass under the second connecting thread (shown in red) and up through the second bead of the set (figure 21).

3 Continue with brick stitch, adding one bead at a time.

4 At the end of the row, pick up one bead and pass down through the fifth bead in the first row, up through the fourth bead in the first row, and up through the third bead in the second row (figure 22).

5 Pass down through the fourth bead in the second row and up through the last bead in the second row (figure 23).

6 For the next row, pick up two beads and pass under the first connecting thread (shown in red in figure 24) and up through the second bead in the set. Continue with brick stitch to complete the row.

7 Begin the next row by picking up two beads and passing under the second connecting thread as done in step 2 (refer to figure 21). Repeat steps 3 through 5 to complete the row.

8 Repeat steps 6 and 7, alternating between passing under the first and second connecting loops to begin the rows.

Square Stitch

This strong stitch is useful in beadwork. Because it mimics loom work, you can use needlework patterns with it. Its downside is that it takes some time to do.

1 String on a stopper bead (shown in orange in the figures) and pick up the requisite number of beads for the base row (five are used in the example).

2 Pick up one bead (green 1 in figure 25) and pass through the corresponding bead in the base row (purple 1) from left to right, then pass through the bead just added again.

3 Continue adding beads to the base row as in step 1 (figure 26).

4 Pass through all the beads in the previous row, then pass through all the beads in the current row (figure 27). This tightens the tension.

Repeat steps 3 and 4 as needed.

16

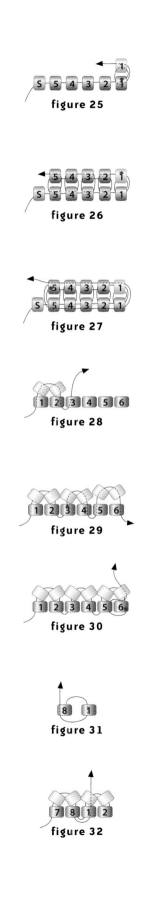

figure 25

figure 26

figure 27

figure 28

figure 29

figure 30

figure 31

figure 32

Herringbone Stitch

Herringbone is a relatively easy and quick stitch that derives its name from the herringbone pattern it resembles when completed. It can be worked in flat, tubular, and circular forms.

Flat Herringbone Stitch

1 Begin by making a bead ladder (page 15) with an even number of beads (six are used in the example). This is the base row for the stitch.

2 With the thread exiting bead 1 (figure 28), pick up two beads and pass down through bead 2 and up through bead 3.

3 Pick up two beads and pass down through bead 4 and up through bead 5. Pick up two more beads and pass down through bead 6 (figure 29).

4 To get into position for the next row, pass up through bead 5 in the base row and up through the last bead added (figure 30).

Repeat steps 2 through 4 as needed.

Tubular Herringbone Stitch

1 Make a bead ladder (page 15) with an even number of beads (eight are used in the example). Join the last bead to the first bead to form a tube (figure 31).

2 Follow the instructions for flat herringbone stitch (page 17) to complete the row. After adding the last two beads, pass up through two beads (figure 32). This is the step up for tubular herringbone.

Repeat step 2 until the tube is the desired length, remembering to step up at the end of every row.

Right Angle Weave

Right angle weave is an extremely versatile stitch. It has a drapelike quality that is perfect for many designs. It can also be made into structural components by folding the pieces and adding beads in the ditches to make them firm. The best way to learn right angle weave is to practice using two alternating colors.

Flat Right Angle Weave

1 Pick up four beads and pass through them again to form a circle (figure 33).

2 Pick up three beads and pass down through bead 4, then up through beads 5 and 6 (figure 34).

3 Pick up three beads and pass up through bead 6, then down through beads 8 and 9 (figure 35). To complete the base row in the practice piece, pick up three beads and pass down through bead 9 and up through beads 11, 12, and 13. With the thread exiting bead 13, you're in position to begin the next row. Notice that you're making units by alternating clockwise and counterclockwise thread paths.

figure 33

figure 34

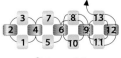

figure 35

4 Pick up three beads; pass through the top bead in the previous row (bead 13), then up through the first bead just added (bead 14), as shown in figure 36. Every row in right angle weave begins with three beads.

5 Pick up two beads; pass through the next bead of the previous row (bead 8), the side bead of the previous unit (bead 14), through the two beads just added (beads 17 and 18), and through the next bead of the previous row (bead 7), as shown in figure 37.

6 Complete the row by picking up two beads for each unit and moving in a clockwise, then counterclockwise, direction (figure 38). For the last unit, pass through only the first bead just added to end in position to begin the next row.

7 With the thread exiting bead 21, pick up three beads (remember three beads are needed to begin each row). Pass through bead 21, through the beads just added (beads 23, 24, and 25), and then through the next bead of the previous row (bead 20), as shown in figure 39.

Continue in this manner until the piece is the desired length.

Tubular Right Angle Weave

There are a few ways to make a tube with right angle weave. My favorite is to make a flat piece and zip it up to form a tube.

1 Refer to figure 40 as you work. Make a flat piece of right angle weave (page 17) that's the desired length and *one unit less* than the desired width. Fold the piece in half lengthwise so the side beads line up as shown in the figure.

2 With the thread exiting bead 1 of the left unit, pick up one bead (shown in purple for purposes of clarification) and pass through the corresponding bead 1 of the right unit.

3 Pick up one bead and pass through bead 1 of the left unit, the first bead added, bead 1 of the right unit, the second bead added, and then down through bead 2 of the left unit.

4 Pick up one bead and pass up through bead 2 of the right unit, the second bead added, bead 2 of the left unit, the bead just added, and then down through bead 3 of the right unit.

Continue in this manner, picking up one bead to complete the unit between the two ends, until the tube is completely joined.

Stitch in the Ditch with Right Angle Weave

With right angle weave, I often stitch in the ditch to embellish the piece or to build a firmer component. With the thread exiting a bead of the right angle weave unit, pick up a bead and pass through the bead in the next unit as shown in figure 41.

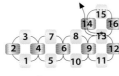

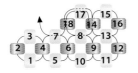

figure 36

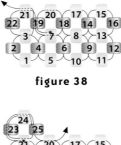

figure 38

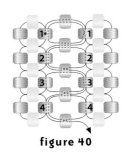

figure 40

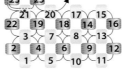

figure 37

figure 39

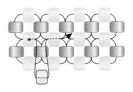

figure 41

Nepal Chain

This lovely stitch can be used to embellish other forms of chain or flat beadwork, or as a base for developing other forms. Combining different sizes of beads will determine the look of the chain.

You'll need two sizes of beads; I almost always use 11° cylinder beads for the stems and 15° or 11° round seed beads for the clusters. You could use small semiprecious stones (2–3 mm) for the clusters, but practice first with seed and cylinder beads, which have more uniform holes.

Tip: Tension is an issue with this stitch. Take care at each step to keep the work taut.

1 Pick up four cylinder beads (shown in blue in figure 42) and five 15°s (shown in orange). Pass down through three of the cylinder beads and into the opposite end of the first cylinder bead. This bead becomes a sort of stopper bead. Make a half-hitch knot here to hold the beadwork in place.

2 Pass through the next three cylinder beads again to get into position to begin the next cluster.

3 Pick up three cylinder beads and five 15°s, pass down through the three cylinder beads just added, and then up through bead 5 of the previous cluster (figure 43).

4 Pick up three cylinder beads and five 15°s, pass down through the three cylinder beads just added, and then up through bead 1 of the previous cluster (figure 44).

Continue in this manner, alternating between passing through bead 5 and bead 1 of the previous cluster, until the chain is the desired length.

St. Petersburg Chain

This chain drapes softly and is quite sturdy. Variations work well as additions to sculptural designs, and you can combine different sizes of beads for a variety of looks. This example uses size 11° cylinder beads and size 15° round seed beads.

1 String on a stopper bead. Pick up four cylinder beads and pass through the first two beads again so the beads lie two-by-two and side by side with the holes facing up and down (figure 45). With the thread exiting the second bead, pick up one 15° and pass through the second set of two beads.

2 Pick up four cylinder beads and pass through the first two beads added so the beads lie two-by-two and side by side.

3 Pick up one 15° and pass down through three cylinder beads (outlined in red in figure 46). Pick up one 15° and pass up through the set of two beads as shown in the figure.

Repeat steps 2 and 3 until the chain is the desired length.

St. Petersburg chain

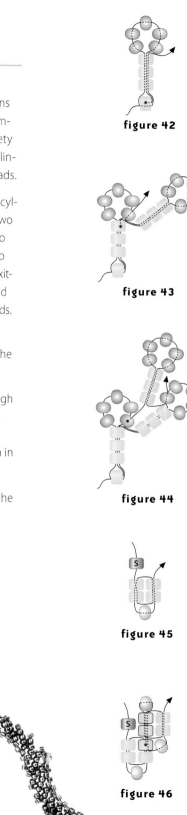

figure 42

figure 43

figure 44

figure 45

figure 46

Backstitch

Backstitch is used primarily in bead embroidery. This is a variation used for embellishment or to cover raw edges in a design.

Backstitch Edging

1 With the thread exiting a bead on the edge of the beadwork, pick up three beads and place them along the edge.

2 Pass through the third bead on the edge as shown in figure 47, then pass through the previous bead on the edge as shown. Pass again through the second and third beads just added.

3 Repeat along the entire edge.

Backstitch Embellishment

Work this the same as for the edging, but instead of passing through beads on an edge, pass through beads in a row or rows of completed beadwork.

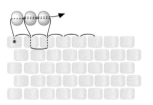

figure 47

Combining Stitches

This is where the fun begins! By combining stitches, design possibilities are endless. Carol Wilcox Wells opened the door for many of us in her first book, *Creative Beadweaving*. The last chapter of that book changed the way I looked at beadwork and design.

Switching from Brick Stitch to Peyote Stitch

1 With the thread exiting a bead in the last row of brick stitch (figure 48), pick up three beads (shown in green in the illustration), pass under the connecting thread (shown in red), and then up through bead 3.

2 Pick up two beads (4 and 5 in figure 49), pass under the next connecting thread (shown in red), and then back up through bead 5.

3 Continue the transition by picking up two beads and passing under the next connecting thread and up through the second bead of the two.

4 When adding the last two transition beads (6 and 7 in figure 50), pass through the second-to-last bead and then the third-to-last bead of the previous row, up through bead 5 added in step 2, and again through bead 6 to be in position to start the next row.

5 The upper beads added in steps 1 through 4 now become the up beads for peyote stitch. Weave over to bead 2 and, with the thread exiting that bead, pick up a bead and pass through bead 4 (figure 51). Continue with peyote stitch for the entire row and step up at the end of the row for even-count peyote stitch (page 13).

Alternative Method for Switching from Brick to Peyote

With the thread exiting a bead in the last row of brick stitch, *pick up one bead (shown in green in figure 52), pass down through the next bead in the row, and then up through the following bead. Repeat from * for the entire row. The new beads added become the up beads for peyote stitch.

figure 48

figure 50

figure 51

figure 49

figure 52

Switching from Right Angle Weave to Peyote Stitch

Switching from right angle weave to peyote is very easy and I often use a base row of right angle weave to start peyote stitch.

The blue beads in figure 53 become the up beads for peyote. With the thread exiting one of these beads, pick up an orange bead and pass through the next bead in the right angle weave row. Repeat for the entire row.

Switching from Peyote Stitch to Brick Stitch

The switch from peyote stitch to brick stitch isn't as simple as the transition for the stitches previously described. I usually use a size 12 Sharps needle for this technique—the shorter length makes it easier to get between two beads to catch a thread.

1 With the thread exiting a bead on the piece of peyote stitch, pick up two beads (remember the cardinal rule that every row of brick stitch begins with two beads) and catch the thread (shown in red) between the two peyote beads (figure 54). Pass up through the second bead of the two just added. The two beads should lie side by side with the holes facing up and down.

2 Pick up one bead, catch the next thread in the peyote stitch, and pass through the bead just added (figure 55).

Repeat step 2 until you have the number of beads needed to set up the base row for brick stitch.

Switching from Square Stitch to Brick Stitch

This transition is made along one of the sides of a square stitch piece—an edge with threads showing. With the thread exiting a bead on one of those edges, pick up two beads (again, the cardinal rule in brick stitch: every row begins with two beads), pass under the connecting thread, and then up through the second bead as shown in figure 56, so that the beads lie side by side with the holes facing up and down. *Pick up one bead, pass under the next connecting thread, and then up through the bead just added. Repeat from * to complete the row.

Switching from Square Stitch to Peyote Stitch or Right Angle Weave

This transition is made along one of the sides of a square stitch piece, where the threads show on an edge.

1 With the thread exiting a bead on one of the side edges, pick up three beads, pass under the connecting thread, and then up through the third bead added (figure 57).

2 Pick up two beads (4 and 5 in figure 58), pass under the next connecting thread (shown in red), and then back up through bead 5.

3 Continue the transition by picking up two beads and passing under the next connecting thread and then up through the second bead of the two.

4 The upper beads added in steps 1 through 3 now become the up beads for peyote stitch, or the lower beads in units of right angle weave.

figure 53

figure 54

figure 55

figure 56

figure 57

figure 58

CHAPTER THREE

ANCIENT & ANTIQUE JEWELRY AS INSPIRATION

I remember the exact moment a piece of ancient jewelry became a point of inspiration. I was at an exhibit of finds excavated from the first-century eruption of Vesuvius that buried Pompeii, Herculaneum, and the surrounding areas. One of the cases contained a gold bracelet made with granulation. The granules were joined to form domes about an inch (2.5 cm) across, joined with gold rings. The minute I saw this, a vision of size-15 round seed beads stitched with circular brick stitch popped into my head. I immediately looked for something to write on but all I had was the back of my checkbook. (I now try to remember to carry a small sketchpad!)

The exhibit also featured a necklace with open gold work from Oplonti, and I thought of right angle weave with peyote-bezeled stones. I couldn't get home fast enough. Upon arriving, I pulled out my beads and the doors opened.

These flashes of insight haven't always come so easily, so I consider that moment a gift from the gods. From then on, I began looking at photos or actual pieces of ancient jewelry to figure out how to interpret them with seed beads. At first I wanted my work to replicate the original piece, but I soon learned that seed beads are a different medium, so what became important to me was to capture the essence and the memory of the original.

VINEYARD

Pio Castellani is one of the masters of nineteenth-century Archaeological Revival Jewelry, the style based on the many archaeological discoveries during the eighteenth and nineteenth centuries and the period of the Grand Tour, when young, upper-class men took a tour of European heritage sites. Souvenirs from a tour often included jewelry, small tobacco boxes, and paintings made of micromosaics. Castellani's style was inspired by ancient Egyptian, Roman, and Etruscan jewelry. This necklace pays homage to his work.

▶ Leaves

1 Using cylinder beads, make a central spine with seven units of right angle weave.

2 Weave back down to the center unit, shown with beads outlined in red in figure 1. Working from the left bead of the center unit, add an arm of five right angle weave units. Weave back to the center unit.

3 Working from the right bead of the center unit, add another arm of five right angle weave units. *Do not weave back to the center unit.* Notice the exit point shown in figure 1. ***Tip:*** To keep the tension the same as the center spine and the other arm, pass through each unit twice when stitching.

SUPPLIES

Basic Beading Kit (page 11)

Size 11° green/gold cylinder beads, 10 g

25 g of amethyst/gold drop beads, 3.4 mm

16 dark purple rounds beads, 4 mm

Size 15° gold metallic round beads, < 1 g

S-hook with jump ring closure

FINISHED SIZE

22½ inches (57.2 cm) long

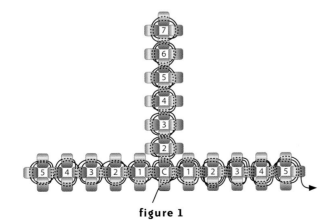

figure 1

The base row of right angle weave is the perfect setup for peyote stitch, which is used for the rest of the leaf. Start by adding the curve to the bottom of the leaf.

Refer to figure 2 for steps 4 through 8.

4 With the thread exiting the bead with the red star, pick up one bead and pass through the next bead in the right angle weave unit (unit 5).

5 Pick up two beads and pass through the low bead in the next right angle weave unit (unit 4).

6 Repeat step 5 two more times, first exiting the low bead of unit 3, then of unit 2.

7 Pick up one bead and pass through the low bead of unit 1. Weave through the center unit to exit the low bead of unit 1 on the other arm. Repeat the pattern *in reverse* to complete the second arm.

8 Weave through the last unit to exit the top bead.

▶ First Half of Leaf

Row 1

Refer to figure 3 for steps 1 through 4.

1 Continue with peyote stitch along the top of the left arm, adding one bead in each spot, for a total of four beads.

2 Pass through the side bead of unit 2 of the center spine *without* a bead. This is the seam between the arm and the spine, and a decrease begins to pull the leaf together.

3 Continue with peyote up to the top of the spine by adding one bead in each spot, for a total of five beads.

4 Catch the thread shown in red in the diagram and pass back through the last two beads exited, making a U-turn; this decrease shapes the tip of the leaf.

Row 2

Refer to figure 4 for steps 1 through 5.

1 Peyote stitch back down to the center, adding a total of four beads.

2 Work the seam decrease by passing through the next bead of the left arm without adding a bead.

3 Pick up one bead and pass through the next up bead.

4 Decrease in the next spot by passing directly through the next up bead. This will dramatically pull the piece into shape.

5 Add one bead in the next spot.

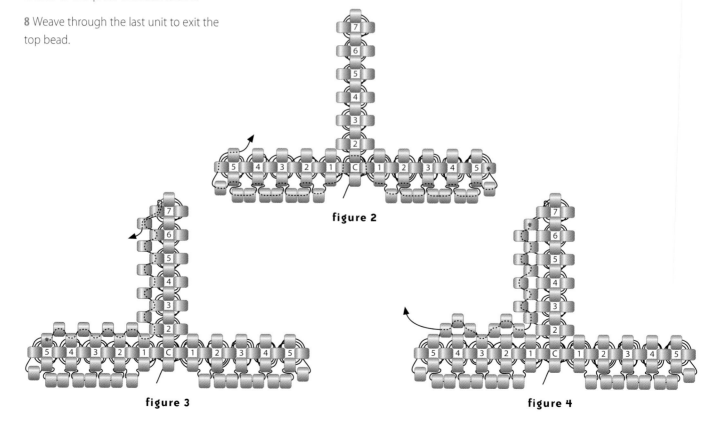

figure 2

figure 3

figure 4

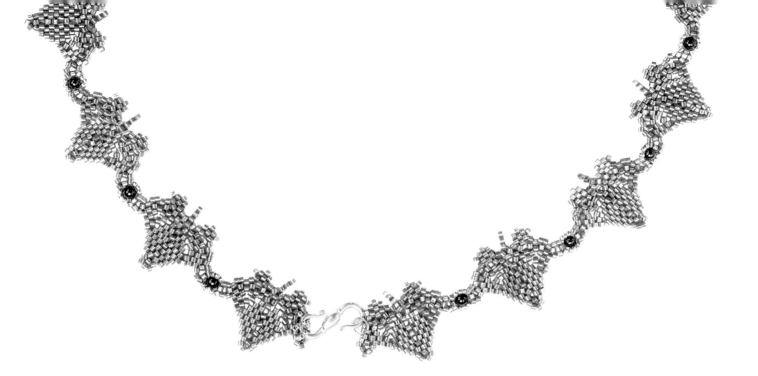

Row 3

Refer to figure 5 for rows 3 through 5.

1 Pick up one bead and make a regular flat peyote turn by passing back through the last bead added in row 2. Row 3 is marked R3 in the diagram, with the beads outlined in red.

2 Place one bead in the decrease spot as shown.

3 Work the seam decrease by passing through the next up bead on the center spine.

4 Continue to peyote stitch one bead in each spot for a total of three beads.

5 Catch a thread between rows 1 and 2 and make a U-turn, passing through the last two beads exited.

Row 4

1 Peyote stitch two beads in row 4, which is marked R4 and outlined in purple.

2 Work the seam decrease by passing through the next up bead of the arm, then work one more peyote stitch on the arm.

Row 5

1 Pick up one bead and make a regular flat peyote turn as previously done at the beginning of row 3.

2 Decrease at the seam by passing through the second bead added in row 4.

3 Place one bead, catch a thread, and make a U-turn.

4 Ladder stitch the two beads added in row 5 to complete the first half.

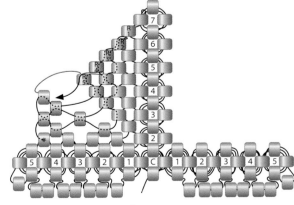

figure 5

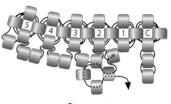

figure 6

▶ Second Half of Leaf

1 Weave through the beadwork to exit the top bead of the fifth unit on the right arm.

2 Repeat rows 1 through 5 of First Half of Leaf to complete the second half of the leaf.

Refer to figure 6 for steps 3 and 4.

3 Ladder stitch two beads to the center unit to create the stem of the leaf (outlined in red).

4 With the thread exiting the bead identified by a red star in the illustration, pick up one bead and pass through the first bead of the next set of two beads, splitting the pair. Pick up two beads and pass back through the first bead added in this step. Weave over to the same point on the other side of the spine and repeat this step.

Repeat all steps to make 17 leaves for a 20-inch (50.8 cm) necklace. Set aside.

▶ Grape Clusters

The clusters are made with a variation of Nepal chain. Once you make the base, you'll add more grapes with freeform shaping.

1 Using cylinder beads for the stems and drops for the grapes, make a base of six groups of Nepal chain as shown in figure 7.

2 Fold unit 5 over on top of unit 6. This sets up the tapered bottom of the cluster. Tack the units together by attaching beads in unit 5 to beads in unit 6 (figure 8). Pay attention to the thread path, making sure that not too much thread shows.

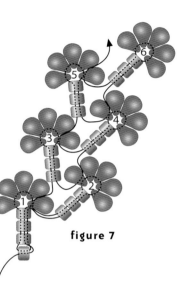

figure 7

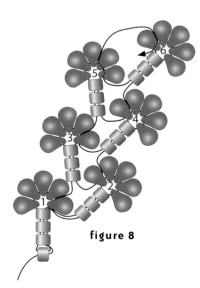

figure 8

3 You'll now use freeform shaping to make clusters that are fuller at the top than at the bottom. (Holding the piece flat between your thumb and forefinger helps when shaping the piece.) Pick up two beads and pass through one of the drop beads in the fourth cluster (figure 9). Continue shaping the cluster by adding one or two beads at a time, working up to the top of the cluster. Weave through the beadwork to exit the last bead on the stem.

Repeat steps 1 through 3 to make seven or nine clusters for the necklace.

▶ Join Clusters to Leaves

With the needle exiting the last bead on the stem of a cluster, align this bead with a bead of the right angle weave unit of the center spine of a leaf, as shown in figure 10. Place the cluster on top of the leaf and ladder stitch the two beads together. Continue to stitch the beads of the stem to the center spine of the leaf until the cluster is securely attached to the leaf. Repeat to attach each cluster to a leaf.

▶ Assemble the Necklace

The leaves and cluster are joined with the 4-mm beads and figure-eight joins.

1 With the thread exiting the top of an end bead of a leaf (figure 11), pick up two cylinder beads, one 4-mm bead, and three cylinder beads. Pass through the corresponding end bead of another leaf from bottom to top. Pick up two cylinder beads, pass back through the 4-mm bead, pick up three cylinder beads, and pass through the original end bead from bottom to top.

2 Pass through the first two cylinder beads added and through the 4-mm bead. Pick up three 15°s and pass through the 4-mm bead again in the same direction, so the 15°s hug the top of the 4-mm bead. Pick up three more 15°s and pass through the 4-mm bead again so that these 15°s hug the bottom of the bead.

3 Weave through the beadwork and through the end bead on the second leaf. Reinforce, knot, and tie off.

Repeat for each leaf, centering the grape clusters in the necklace.

▶ Closure

Attach one end of the S-hook to one of the end leaves with two loops of 15°s. Stitch the ring to the other end leaf.

Don't want to make all 17 leaves and clusters for a necklace? Just bead a pair and use them as earrings.

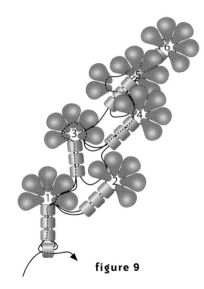

figure 9

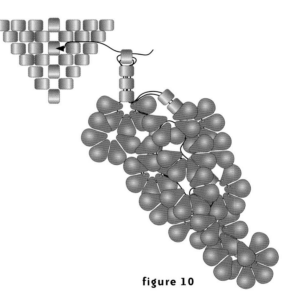

figure 10

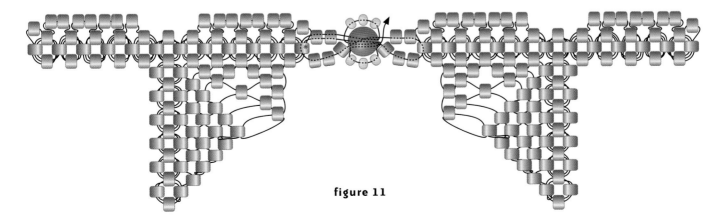

figure 11

MATRIARCHS' CUFF

A Jewish marriage ring I saw at *Bedazzled: 5,000 Years of Jewelry*, an exhibit at the Walters Art Museum in Baltimore, Maryland, provides the inspiration for this cuff. Many of these rings are adorned with houses and roofs. The ornate ring I've mimicked—dating to the seventeenth or eighteenth century—has filigree rosettes, enameled leaves, and a blue enameled tower that opens to reveal a small gold plate with the first two letters of *mazel tov* engraved on it. The cuff is named for the four Jewish matriarchs: Sarah, Rebekah, Rachel, and Leah.

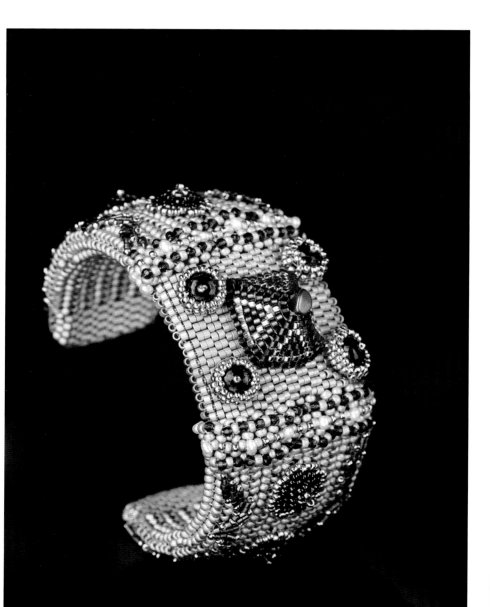

SUPPLIES

Basic Beading Kit (page 11)

Size 11° round seed beads, Color A, matte gold, 15 g

Size 11° cylinder beads:

   Color A, matte gold, 7 g

   Color B, cobalt blue, 2 g

   Color C, metallic gold, 1 g

Size 15° round seed beads:

   Color C, metallic gold, 2 g

   Color D, ruby red, 2 g

Size 15° cylinder beads, matte green, 1 g

4 round semiprecious rondelles, dark red, 6 mm

60 round Swarovski crystals, smoky blue, 2 mm

6 seed pearls, 2 mm

1 brass cuff blank with center square indent, 7 inches by 1½ inches (17.8 x 3.8 cm)

FINISHED SIZE

1½ inches (3.8 cm) at widest point

2⅝ inches (6.7 cm) tall when standing

▶ Cuff Sides

You'll make two tubular herringbone stitch sections for the sides, then join them around the brass blank to a center section of two-drop peyote stitch.

Row 1 Make a 32-bead ladder using 11° rounds. Join the last bead in the ladder to the first bead in the ladder to form a tube.

Rows 2–13 Next, continue with 11° rounds and complete 13 rows of tubular herringbone, stepping up at the end of each row. It's important to check the fit of the tube on the blank every few rows. Slide the piece onto the blank with the beginning bead ladder toward the center of the blank.

Row 14 Begin to decrease on the edges of the cuff. Pick up one bead and pass through the second bead of the set in the previous row. Continue with regular herringbone for seven units of two beads. At the other edge of the cuff, pick up one bead and pass through the second bead of the next set as you did at the beginning of the row (figure 1).

Complete the row with seven more two-bead units of regular herringbone. To step up, pass through the first bead of the herringbone set in row 13, through the one-bead decrease, down into the second bead of the row 13 herringbone set, and up through two beads—the next bead in row 13 and the next bead in row 14 (figure 2).

Row 15 Continue with herringbone for seven units. At the edge of the cuff, pass directly through the one-bead unit (figure 3), add seven more units, and then pass directly through the one-bead unit on the other edge and step up.

Row 16 Add one bead on each edge and seven units of regular herringbone on each side, between the edges. Remember to check the fit on the brass blank every few rows. The decrease edges should lie on the edges of the blank.

Row 17 Repeat row 15.

Row 18 Repeat row 16.

Rows 19–22 Work 16 units of regular tubular herringbone without the one-bead decreases.

Rows 23–26 Switch to 11° cylinder As and continue with tubular herringbone.

Row 27 Work single-bead peyote stitch, placing one bead in each two-bead herringbone spot. Step up at the end of the row through the first bead added.

Row 28 Work two-bead peyote stitch, adding two beads between the single beads in row 27 (figure 4). Step up at the end of the row.

Row 29 Repeat row 27.

Row 30 Repeat row 28 but decrease on both edges by placing one bead in the peyote spot.

Final rows The fit is most important in the final rows, so check it after every row. Continue with the two-bead/one-bead peyote pattern, decreasing on the edges as needed. **_Tip:_** I often work this portion right on the blank. Zip the ends together.

figure 1

figure 3

figure 2

figure 4

Right Angle Weave Join

You'll now set up the edge on the open end of the component for converting to right angle weave, which you'll use to join the sides to the center of the cuff.

Row 1 Using 11° rounds and starting at an edge, do the following steps for a total of 32 up beads.

1 With the thread exiting a bead in the last row of herringbone stitch (figure 5), pick up three beads, pass under the connecting thread (shown in red), and up through bead 3.

2 Pick up two beads (beads 4 and 5 in figure 6), then pass under the next connecting thread (shown in red) and back up through bead 5.

3 Continue the transition by picking up two beads and passing under the next connecting thread and up through the second bead of the two.

Step up through the last up bead of the row.

Rows 2 and 3 Work two rows of tubular right angle weave. **Note:** When working in the round, only one bead is needed at the end of the round to complete the last unit.

Row 4 Complete 16 units of right angle weave on what will become the outside of the cuff.

Set the component aside and repeat all steps to make the component for the other side of the cuff.

▶ Center Section

This section is made using flat two-drop peyote stitch and fits around the center portion of the cuff.

Rows 1 and 2 String on a stopper bead followed by 56 size 11° cylinder As. *Pick up two beads, skip two beads, and pass through the next two beads. Repeat from * for the entire row. You'll end up with 28 sets of two beads.

Rows 3–35 Continue with two-drop peyote until you have 35 complete rows. Set the piece aside.

figure 5

figure 6

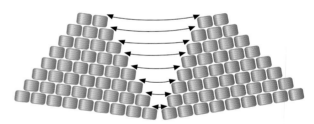

figure 7

▶ Focal Decoration

The decoration is added to the center section prior to attaching it to the center of the blank.

Triangle Dome

This component is made of four flat triangles made with brick stitch that are joined to form the dome.

Row 1 Make a ladder using nine cylinder Bs.

Rows 2–8 Follow the color pattern in figure 5 to complete eight rows of flat brick stitch.

Repeat rows 1 through 8 to make a total of four triangles. Ladder stitch the four triangles together as shown in figure 7.

Center the triangle dome on the flat peyote piece and tack it down by pass-ing through beads or catching threads on the peyote base. Attach the rondelles to the flat peyote piece at each point of the dome, and bezel around them using 15° C rounds as follows: *With the thread exiting the beadwork at the base of a rondelle, pick up two or three beads and pass back into the beadwork so the beads are snug against the base of the rondelle. Repeat from * until you have a ring of 15°s around the base of the rondelle. Step up through the first bead added and work several rows of peyote stitch to capture the rondelle.

Gently fold the peyote piece so the focal decorations are centered over the center front of the blank. Join the two ends on the back of the cuff, securing through beads in every row.

▶ Attach the Side Pieces

1 Slide a side piece onto the cuff and zip it to the center section on the front with right angle weave, as shown in figure 8.

2 Zip the backs of the cuff with peyote stitch zip, as shown in figure 9. (This stitch works better because of the curvature of the blank.)

Repeat steps 1 and 2 on the other side. Embellish the right angle weave rows—with crystals, 15° C rounds, and small seed pearls—by stitching in the ditch.

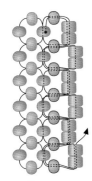

figure 8

figure 9

► Embellish

1 Using 15° rounds, make six rosettes as follows:

Row 1 String four C beads and make a circle by stepping up through the first bead strung.

Row 2 Work peyote stitch, adding one D bead between each of the four beads in row 1. Step up through the first bead added in this row.

Row 3 *Pick up two D beads and pass through one bead in row 2 as shown in figure 10. Repeat from * to complete the row. Step up through the first two beads added in this row.

Row 4 *Pick up one D bead and pass through two beads (treat two beads as one). Repeat from * to complete the row. Step up through the first bead added in this row (figure 11).

Row 5 *Pick up two D beads and pass through one bead as was previously done in row 3. Repeat from * to complete the row. Step up through the first bead only added in this row, splitting the pair (figure 12).

Row 6 *Pick up one bead and pass through the second bead in the pair. Pick up one D and pass through the first bead in the next pair. Repeat from * to complete the row. Step up through the first bead added in this row (figure 13).

Row 7 *Pick up two Ds and pass through one bead in row 6. Repeat from * to complete the row. Step up through the first two beads added in this row.

Row 8 *Pick up one C bead and pass through the next pair in row 7. Repeat from * to complete the row. Step up through the first bead added in this row.

Row 9 *Pick up three C beads and pass through one bead in row 8. Repeat from * to complete the row.

2 Center and attach three rosettes to each side of the cuff.

3 Make eight sections of double St. Petersburg chain using 15° cylinders and 15° C rounds: Make four sections with six rows on each side and four sections with three rows on each side.

4 Drape the chain along the edges of the cuff, placing the longer chains at the widest parts of the cuff and the smaller chains at the ends of the cuff. Tack the chains down by passing through beads on the cuff.

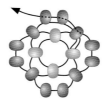

figure 10

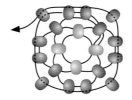

figure 11

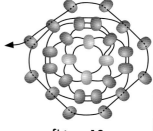

figure 12

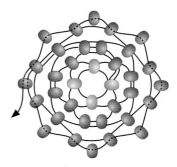

figure 13

ANTONIA EARRINGS

Women in the Antonius family, one of the most influential and wealthy plebian families of ancient Rome, were called Antonia. The name means beautiful, praiseworthy, priceless. These earrings echo the gold work of the Etruscans. This design combines rosettes with right angle weave tubes. The earrings are then embellished with rows of seed bead peyote stitch and semiprecious drops.

SUPPLIES

Basic Beading Kit (page 11)

Size 11° cylinder beads:

Color A, matte gold, 3 g

Color B, amethyst, 1 g

Color C, ivory, 1 g

Size 15° round seed beads:

Color A, matte gold, 5 g

Color D, metallic gold, 1 g

2 faceted amethyst top-drilled drop beads, 6 x 9 mm

2 gold ear wires

FINISHED SIZE

3 inches (7.6 cm) long

figure 1

figure 2

figure 3

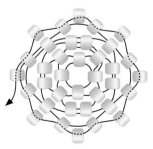

figure 4

► Columns

1 Using 11° cylinder A beads, make four rosettes as follows:

Front

Row 1 String four cylinder beads and make a circle by stepping up through the first bead strung.

Row 2 Work peyote stitch, adding one bead between each of the four beads in row 1. Step up through the first bead added in this row.

Row 3 *Pick up two beads and pass through one bead in row 2 as shown in figure 1. Repeat from * to complete the row. Step up through the first two beads added in this row.

Row 4 *Pick up one bead and pass through two beads (treat two beads as one). Repeat from * to complete the row. Step up through the first bead added in this row (figure 2).

Row 5 *Pick up two beads and pass through one bead as was previously done in row 3. Repeat from * to complete the row. Step up through only the first bead added in this row, splitting the pair (figure 3).

Row 6 *Pick up one bead and pass through the second bead in the pair. Pick up one bead and pass through the first bead in the next pair. Repeat from * to complete the row. Step up through the first bead added in this row (figure 4).

Row 7 *Pick up two beads and pass through one bead in row 6. Repeat from * to complete the row. Step up through the first two beads added in this row.

Row 8 *Pick up one bead and pass through the next pair in row 7. Repeat from * to complete the row. Step up through the first bead added in this row.

Row 9 *Pick up three beads and pass through one bead in row 8. Repeat from * to complete the row. With the front of the rosette complete, you're in position to close the back of the rosette.

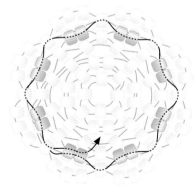

figure 5

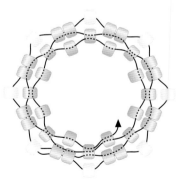

figure 6

Back

Row 1 With the thread exiting a single bead in row 8, *pick up two beads and pass through the next bead in row 8, as shown in figure 5. Repeat from * to complete the row. Step up through the first two beads added in this row. Rows 1 and 2 are shown in figure 6.

Row 2 *Pick up one bead and pass through two beads in row 1. Repeat from * to complete the row. Step up through the first bead added in this row.

Row 3 *Pick up one bead and pass through one bead in row 2. Repeat from * to complete the row. Step up through the first bead added in this row.

Row 4 This row has a gradual decrease. *Pick up one bead, and pass through the next up bead. Then pass through the next down bead and the next up bead, decreasing in this spot. Repeat from * to complete the row, decreasing in every other spot. Step up through the first bead added and the first bead passed through in this row (figure 7).

Row 5 *Pick up one bead and pass through the next up bead, placing one bead in the decrease spot, and weave through to the next decrease spot and repeat. It looks like quite a long distance to travel, but the piece pulls in dramatically and allows the back to remain flat. Repeat from * to complete the row. Pass through the four beads added in this row and tie off the tail thread.

2 Using 15° As, make two right angle weave panels seven units wide and 12 units long. **Note:** Each unit has two beads on the top and bottom and one bead on each side (figure 8).

3 Fold each piece in half lengthwise and zip the sides together to form a tube.

4 Match two 15°s in a right angle weave unit at one end of the tube to a pair of cylinder beads in row 1 of the back of the rosette (the cylinder beads outlined in red in figure 9). Make a right angle weave unit using one 15° on each side (also outlined in red in figure 9).

5 Continue zipping with right angle weave until the tube end is attached to the underside of the rosette.

6 Repeat steps 4 and 5 to attach the other end of the tube to the rosette.

Repeat steps 4 through 6 for the second earring.

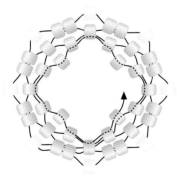

figure 7

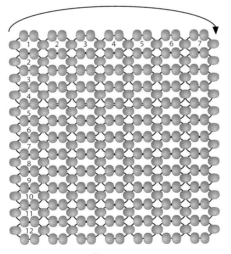

figure 8

figure 9

► Embellish

Beginning at the point where the rosette is attached, build off the tube with peyote stitch, then embellish the rosette with a picot edge, as follows.

Embellish the Tube

Row 1 With the thread exiting a pair of 15°s in row 1 of the tube (figure 10), pick up one cylinder B and pass through the next pair of 15°s. Continue adding one cylinder B through each pair of 15°s to complete the row and step up through the first bead added.

Row 2 Pick up two cylinder Bs and pass through the next cylinder B in row 1. Repeat to complete the row and step up through the first two beads added (figure 11).

Refer to figure 12 for rows 3 through 6 and the rosette embellishment.

Row 3 Pick up one cylinder C and pass through the next pair of cylinder Bs added in row 2. Repeat to complete the row and step up through the first bead added (figure 12).

Row 4 Pick up two cylinder Cs and pass through the next cylinder C added in row 3. Repeat to complete the row and step up through the first two beads added.

Row 5 Pick up one cylinder B and pass through the next two cylinder Cs added in row 4. Repeat to complete the row and step up through the first bead added.

Row 6 Pick up two cylinder Bs and pass through the next cylinder B added in row 5. Repeat to complete the row. Tack this last peyote stitch row to the tube by passing through beads on the tube if possible, or by catching threads in the right angle weave.

Repeat rows 1 through 6 on the other end of the tube and on both ends of the second tube.

Embellish the Rosettes

With the thread exiting a bead in row 8 of the front of a rosette, pick up three 15° Ds and pass through the next bead in row 8 of the rosette. Repeat for the entire row and tie off the thread. Repeat the picot on the other rosette and on the two rosettes of the second earring.

► Finish

1 With the thread exiting a bead at the center of a rosette, pick up two cylinder As, two 15° Ds, one drop, and two 15° Ds. Pass back through the second cylinder A added, pick up one cylinder A, and pass through another bead at the center of the rosette. Repeat on one rosette of the second earring.

2 With the thread exiting a bead at the center of the rosette at the other end, pick up one cylinder A and nine 15° Ds. Pass through an ear wire, back through the cylinder A just added, and into the center of the rosette. Repeat the thread path for added strength. Repeat for the second earring.

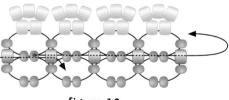

figure 10

figure 11

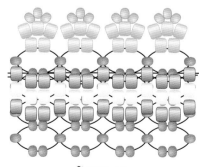

figure 12

OLBIA BRACELET

This bracelet is modeled after a treasure from an ancient Greek colony called Olbia, which was uncovered in Crimea in 1891. I first saw the bracelet in a book and then was fortunate enough to see the original in *Bedazzled: 5,000 Years of Jewelry*, an exhibit at the Walters Art Museum in Baltimore, Maryland. This bracelet combines a multitude of stitches and is an elegant piece to add to your own collection of beaded treasures.

SUPPLIES

Basic Beading Kit (page 11)

Size 15° cut seed beads:

   Color A, matte metallic gold, 10 g

   Color B, shiny metallic gold AB, 5 g

   Color C, lined lilac, 2 g

Size 11° cylinder beads:

   Color A, matte metallic gold, 5 g

   Color D, shiny metallic gold, 1 g

Size 15° green metallic cylinder beads, 5 g

Size 11° round beads:

   Color A, matte metallic gold, < 1 g

   Color D, shiny metallic gold, < 1 g

28 flat round semiprecious beads, 3 mm

4 round ruby beads, 8 mm

1 turquoise cabochon, 20 x 15 mm

12 small gold metallic drop beads

1 gold 5-hole spacer bar clasp

FINISHED SIZE

1½ x 7¾ inches (3.8 x 19.7 cm)

▶ Side Bands

You'll use right angle weave with 15° cuts and 11° cylinders in color A to make two bracelet bands that will flank a 2-inch (5.1 cm) central piece. Each band is 2½ inches (6.4 cm) long. **Note:** These dimensions are for a 7-inch (17.8 cm) bracelet. If more or less length is needed, make the base row longer or shorter.

1 Make a right angle weave unit with three 15° As, one 11° cylinder A, three 15° As, and one 11° cylinder A, treating the sets of three 15° beads as one. Continue to make a base row that measures 2½ inches (6.4 cm).

2 Complete seven rows of right angle weave as shown in figure 1.

3 After completing the seven rows, stitch in the right angle weave ditch using 15° As as shown in figure 2. Notice that there are no beads in the ditches between rows 3 and 4, or 4 and 5. This keeps the band wide enough to accommodate the leaf motifs.

Repeat steps 1 through 3 to make another band.

▶ Decorate the Bands

The bands are decorated with small leaves, a variation of St. Petersburg chain, and bezeled semiprecious stones. You'll attach the components to the band by passing through a bead in the component and the bead in the band that lies directly beneath it. This is repeated until the components are firmly attached. Figure 3 shows the placement of the decorative elements.

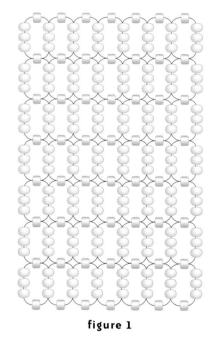

figure 1

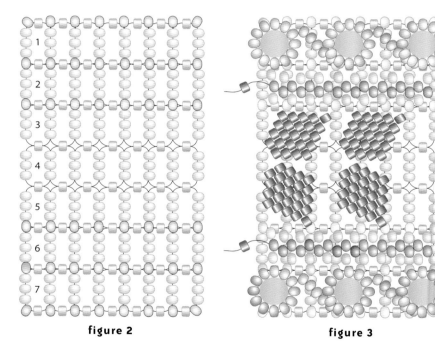

1
2
3
4
5
6
7

figure 2

figure 3

Wave

This element is worked directly on rows 1 and 7 of the band.

1 With the thread exiting the center bead of a right angle weave unit on the band, as shown in figure 4, pick up one semiprecious stone, pass through the corresponding center bead in the unit as shown, back through the focal bead, and through the opposite end of the original bead exited to complete a figure-eight anchor.

2 Refer to figure 5 for all parts of this step. Backstitch around the stone with 15° Bs. Secure the bezel by passing through the 15°s again, and exit as shown. Pick up six 15° Bs, attach them to the base, and exit the middle bead of the band as shown.

Repeat steps 1 and 2 for the length of the band, and then repeat on the other side. Repeat all steps on the second band.

Leaf Motifs

The leaves are made with the 15° cylinder beads using flat brick stitch. A total of 28 leaves are needed for the bracelet, 14 on each band; make them as follows:

Make a bead ladder of five beads. Following the pattern in figure 6, complete one half of the leaf and weave back to the base row to begin the other half.

Repeat to make a total of 28 leaves. With the thread exiting the bead at the bottom of a leaf—the tip with the single bead— lay the leaf at an angle at one end of the band, with the bottom bead placed on row 4. Pass through the bead on the base that lies directly beneath the bottom of the leaf. Pass through a bead on the leaf and then through the bead on the base that lies under it. Repeat until the entire leaf is firmly attached to the base. Turn the base upside down and attach another leaf that is angled in the opposite direction with the bottom of the leaf on row 3. Continue to attach 12 more leaves, evenly spaced along these lines.

St. Petersburg Decoration

Make four strips—two for each band— using a variation of St. Petersburg chain as follows. Each strip is 2½ inches (6.4 cm) long.

1 String on a stopper bead and pick up two 15° Cs (*not* the usual four beads used in such a chain). Pass through the first bead of the pair.

2 Pick one 15° B and pass back down into the first 15° C of the pair. Pick up one 15° B and pass through the second 15° C of the pair (figure 7). Continue until the chain measures 2½ inches (6.4 cm).

3 Lay the chain on the base along the second row of right angle weave. With the thread exiting the end 15° B on one side of the strip, pass through the first 11° cylinder bead on the band. *Pick up one 15° B, pass through the next 15° B on the chain, and then pass through the next 11° cylinder on the base. Repeat from * until the strip is attached along one side, and then secure it along the other side in the same manner.

Repeat steps 1 through 3 to make and attach a total of four strips, two for each band, attached to the second and sixth rows of right angle weave.

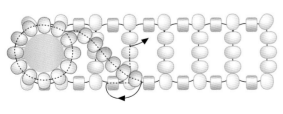

figure 4

figure 5

1 2 3 4 5

figure 6

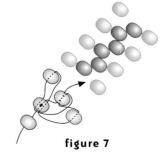

figure 7

▶ Central Piece

This consists of two small bands with rubies and a center band with a bezeled cabochon.

Small Bands

1 String on a stopper bead, followed by 28 size 11° cylinder As. Complete 12 rows of 2-drop peyote stitch. Line this small band up with one of the side bands as shown in figure 8, and zip the pieces together with peyote stitch.

2 Place two rubies on a small band as shown and attach them with a figure-eight anchor. Backstitch around the stones with 15° Bs.

Repeat steps 1 and 2 for the second band.

Center Band

String on a stopper bead followed by 28 size 11° cylinder As. Complete 29 rows of 2-drop peyote stitch.

▶ Cabochon

The cabochon is bezeled with right angle weave using 11° cylinder Ds and 15° Bs. I like to use right angle weave to bezel cabochons because the resulting fabric has the flexibility to fit neatly around the stone.

1 Using 11° cylinder Ds, make a strip of right angle weave to fit around the cabochon. The number of units required depends on the size of your stone—the strip shouldn't be too loose or too tight. Stop one unit short of what's necessary for a good fit. Join the strip into a tube by folding it in half and completing the end unit.

2 Continue with a second row of right angle weave. When you come to the end of the row, you'll only need one bead to close the circle.

3 Depending on the height of your cabochon, you may or may not need another row. Once you have enough rows to fit over the top of the cabochon by one bead,

work a row of peyote stitch, using 15°s to hug the cabochon snugly.

4 Center the bezeled stone on the center band and attach it to the beadwork. Embellish with 11° A rounds by stitching in the ditch around the join. Add a picot of three drop beads to each corner.

Join the Bands

Zip the center band to the small bands using 11° D rounds and right angle weave, as shown in figure 8.

▶ Closure

Center one half of the closure along one end of the bracelet. With the thread exiting a bead on the edge of the bracelet, pass through the first hole of the spacer bar, *pick up one 11° D round, pass back through the hole of the spacer bar and into a bead on the edge of the bracelet. Repeat from * through the next four holes, then attach the other half of the clasp to the other end of the bracelet in the same manner.

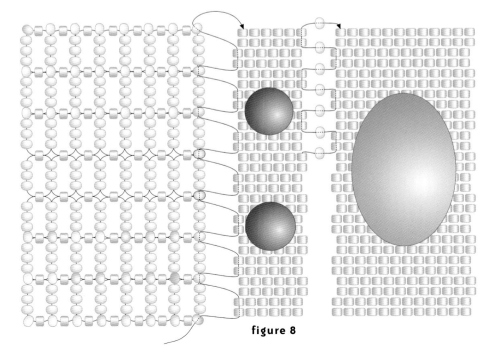

figure 8

GIRANDOLE EARRINGS

Girandole earrings were popular in seventeenth-century Europe. The amount of gold and silver used to make them, and the number of precious gems that adorned them, made them extremely large and heavy. I modeled these on the center of an earring that had a bow motif with three pear-shaped drops. This seed bead design captures the essence of that earring without the weight or the high cost of precious gems.

SUPPLIES

Basic Beading Kit (page 11)

Size 11° silver cylinder beads, 5 g

Size 15° silver round seed beads, 3 g

4 round faceted onyx beads, 4 mm

90 seed pearls, 2 mm

6 pear-shaped freshwater pearls with an up/down hole, approximately 6–8 x 10–12 mm

90 semiprecious black beads, 2 mm

2 silver ear wires

Flat-nosed pliers

FINISHED SIZE

3 inches (7.6 cm) long

► Square Top

The square top is made with circular peyote stitch. It's true, I promise! Figure 1 illustrates rows 1 through 8; the red outlined beads indicate the first bead and the step up at the end of each row. Cylinder beads are used throughout.

Row 1 Pick up four cylinder beads and pass through them again to form a circle. Step up through the first bead strung.

Row 2 Pick up one bead and pass through the next bead in row 1. Repeat three more times, for a total of four beads for the row. Step up through the first bead added in the row.

Row 3 Pick up two beads and pass through the next bead in row 2. Repeat three more times, for a total of eight beads (four sets of two) for the row. Step up through the first bead added, splitting the pair.

Row 4 *Pick up one bead and pass through the second bead in the pair. Pick up one bead and pass through the first bead of the next pair in row 3. Repeat from * three more times, for a total of eight beads in the row. Step up through the first bead added.

Row 5 The setup for the square shape begins now. *Pick up two beads and pass through the next bead in row 4, then pick up one bead and pass through the next bead in row 4. Repeat from * to complete the row. Step up through the first two beads added in the row.

Row 6 Continue with a row of singular peyote, picking up one bead and passing through the next bead, then picking up one bead and passing through the next two beads, treating the two beads as one. Step up through the first bead added in the row.

Row 7 *Pick up one bead and pass through the next bead in row 6; pick up four beads and pass through the next bead in row 6. Repeat from * three times to complete the row. Step up through the first bead added in this row.

Row 8 *Weave over to the four-bead corner and pass through the first two corner beads; pick up one bead and pass through the next two corner beads. Repeat from * to complete three more corners.

► Bow Component

1 Continuing with cylinder beads, repeat rows 1 through 4 of the Square Top.

2 To make the bow, you'll switch to right angle weave. With the thread exiting an up bead in row 4, pick up three beads and pass through the same bead in row 4 to make the first unit. Make two additional right angle weave units (figure 2).

3 Repeat step 2 three more times, beginning at the points shown in figure 3, for a total of four spines.

figure 1

figure 2

figure 3

4 With the thread exiting the end bead of one of the spines, pass through the end bead of the adjacent spine and pull the two spines together. Pick up three beads and pass through the first bead to complete a right angle unit. Repeat with the two spines on the other side of the bow (figure 4).

5 Add two additional right angle weave spines as shown in figure 5, and join together as you did in step 4.

▶ Embellish

You'll embellish the square and the bow with the 15°s, onyx, and seed pearls. The embellishments add color and create the curve in the bow.

Embellish the Centers

1 Place an onyx in the center of the top square component using a figure-eight anchor.

2 With the thread exiting a bead in row 1 of the top square, pick up two 15°s and pass through the next bead in row 1. Repeat to add a total of four sets of two beads. At the end of the row, step up through the first two beads added. Pick up one bead and pass through the next set of two; repeat three times. You now have a ring of 15°s around the onyx (figure 6).

3 With the thread exiting a bead in row 4 as shown in figure 7, *pick up one 15°, one seed pearl, and one 15°, and then pass through the next bead in row 4. Weave through the beadwork to exit the next bead in row 4. Repeat from * three more times.

Repeat steps 1 and 2 at the center of the bow.

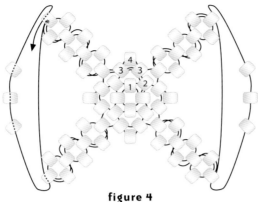

figure 4

figure 5

figure 6

figure 7

Embellish the Bow Spines

1 With the thread exiting a bead on the inner edge of a spine, *pick up one 15° and pass through the next bead on the inner spine. Repeat from * for the entire section (figure 8). **Note:** To keep the illustration clear, it shows only one spine. Each spine will have been joined to an adjacent spine at the top, and you'll embellish the entire inside edge of all three triangular shapes.

2 With the thread exiting a bead on the center row of a spine, pick up one seed pearl and pass through the next bead in the row, following the thread path in figure 8. Repeat to embellish the center rows of all three triangular shapes.

3 With the thread exiting a bead on the outer edge of a spine, pick up one seed pearl and pass through the next bead on the outer edge. Repeat to embellish the outer edges of all three triangular shapes.

▶ Pearl Drops

Each freshwater pearl is surrounded with a right angle weave base row embellished with 2-mm semiprecious stones. Because freshwater pearls can differ in shape and size, use the following instructions as a guideline.

1 Begin with an eight-unit right angle weave base row of cylinder beads. With the thread exiting the top bead of the unit, pass through the freshwater pearl from top to bottom.

2 Anchor the beadwork by passing through the top bead on the other end of the strip, back up through the pearl, and into the opposite end of the seed bead exited. Make sure the strip isn't twisted and lies flat against the pearl.

3 Create another right angle weave unit that covers the top hole of the pearl as shown in figure 9. Continue with right angle weave and complete six additional units.

4 With one strip lying on each side of the pearl, zip the units together at the bottom of the pearl, adding two beads for a new right angle weave unit (figure 10).

5 With the thread exiting a side bead of a unit in the right angle weave strip, pick up one 15° round, and pass through the side bead of the next unit. Continue adding 15°s between each of the beads along this side of the pearl, then weave over to the other side of the pearl and repeat. This helps capture the pearl and tighten the right angle weave rows.

figure 8

figure 9

figure 10

6 With the thread exiting a cylinder bead about two-thirds of the way down the pearl on the right angle weave strip, pick up three cylinder beads to create a new right angle weave unit. Repeat to make a total of six units (figure 11). Weave to the other side and repeat. Zip together the two rows built off of the pearl.

7 Add 2-mm semiprecious stones between the right angle weave units just added on both sides, as you did with 15°s in step 5 (figure 12).

▶ **Assemble**

1 Attach the pearls to the bow as shown in the photo using double loops of 15°s. Using ladder stitch, attach one point of the square to the top of the bow.

2 Using a pair of flat nose pliers, gently turn the loop of an ear wire so that it lies flat against the back of the square component. With the thread exiting a bead at the top of the component, pass through the loop on the ear wire, pick up one 15°, and pass back into the beadwork to hold the ear wire in place. Pick up one or more 15° and pass through the loop and back into the beadwork, continuing until the wire is securely fastened. There's an element of winging it here—just work until the ear wire is secured.

figure 11

figure 12

Here's a very similar version of the Girandole Earrings; besides the obvious color differences, note how I used jump rings to connect the bow to the square top and the dangles.

MACHA

This design has gone through many incarnations. The original piece was inspired by the torques—necklaces of twisted metal wire that are open in the front—worn in ancient Ireland. But as time went on, I fell in love with the spirals found in Celtic designs, and Macha evolved to incorporate spirals and more color. This necklace is named for the woman who was the only High Queen among the High Kings of Ireland.

▶ Spirals

The spirals are made using circular peyote stitch following a two-color pattern. You'll make eight large circles, which will then be joined with peyote stitch to smaller circles to form three-dimensional spiral components.

Large Spirals

Row 1 Pick up three cylinder As and pass through them again to form a circle. Step up through the first bead.

Row 2 Work circular peyote with cylinder B, stepping up at the end of the row.

Row 3 This row is an increase row. Pay particular attention to the color pattern shown in figure 1. Pick up one cylinder A and one cylinder B and pass through the next bead in row 2. Repeat for the entire row to add a total of three sets of two beads (one A, followed by one B). At the end of the row, step up through the first bead added, splitting the pair.

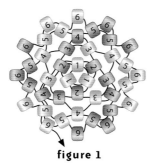

figure 1

SUPPLIES

Basic Beading Kit (page 11)

Size 11° cylinder beads:

   Color A, metallic gold, 15 g

   Color B, dark purple, 15 g

Size 11° round seed beads:

   Color A, metallic gold, 15 g

   Color C, matte gold, 15 g

Size 15° round seed beads:

   Color C, matte gold, < 1 g

2 Swarovski glass pearls, 10 mm

7 Swarovski smoky blue round crystals, 2 mm

1 pear-shaped drop, 20 x 12 mm

Glad Press'n Seal

FINISHED SIZE

Focal element, 3 inches (7.6 cm) wide

7¼ inches (18.4 cm) from spiral edge to spiral edge

through (figure 2). At this point, the spiraling pattern becomes quite evident. Step up through the first bead added.

Row 8 Keeping in the spiral color pattern, work regular peyote without any increases. Step up through the first bead added.

Row 9 This is an increase row. *Pick up two cylinder As and pass through the next up bead; pick up two cylinder As and pass through the next up bead; pick up two cylinder Bs and pass through the next up bead; pick up two cylinder Bs and pass through the next up bead. Repeat from *, adding a total of 12 sets of two beads each. Step up at the end of the row through the first two beads added.

Row 10 Continuing to pick up the same color as the beads you'll be passing through, pick up one bead and pass through the next pair in row 9 (treat two beads as one).

Row 6 *Pick up one cylinder A and pass through the next bead in row 5. Pick up one cylinder B and pass through the first bead of the next pair in row 5. Pick up one cylinder B and pass through the second bead in the pair. Pick up one cylinder A and pass through the first bead of the next pair. Repeat from *, adding a total of 12 beads in the row. Once again, pick up the same color of the bead you'll be passing through. Step up through the first bead added.

Row 7 This is a row of regular peyote without any increases. Once again, pick up the color of the bead you'll be passing

Row 4 This is the second part of the increase. *Pick up one cylinder B and pass through the second bead of the first pair in row 3. Pick up one cylinder A and pass through the first bead of the next pair in row 3. Repeat from * to add a total of six beads for the row, paying attention to the pattern to make the spiral. Step up through the first bead added in the row.

Row 5 This is an increase row. *Pick up two cylinder As and pass through the next bead in row 4. Pick up two cylinder Bs and pass through the next bead in the previous row. Repeat from * to add a total of six sets of two beads. **Tip:** Pick up the same color of the bead you'll be passing through. Step up through the first bead added in the row, splitting the pair.

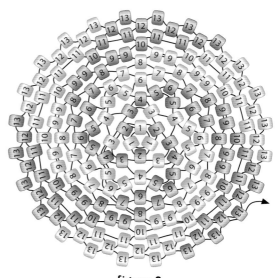

figure 2

Repeat to add a total of 12 beads in this row. Step up at the end of the row through the first bead added.

Row 11 This is an increase row. Continuing in the spiral color pattern, add two beads between each up bead in row 10 to add a total of 12 sets of two beads. Step up at the end of the row through the first bead added, splitting the pair.

Row 12 *Pick up one bead and pass through the second bead of the pair. Pick up one bead and pass through the first bead of the next pair. Repeat from * for the entire row, adding a total of 24 beads. Step up through the first bead added.

Row 13 Work regular peyote without any increases, following the color pattern. Step up through the first bead added.

Repeat rows 1 through 13 to make a total of eight large spirals.

Small Spirals

Three small spirals are needed to make one half of the larger component; you'll need a total of 32 small spirals to complete the necklace. For each small spiral, complete rows 1 through 6 of Large Spiral.

▶ Large Component Halves

Join three small spirals to each large spiral as follows:

Position the two pieces as shown in figure 3. With the thread exiting an outer B bead on the small spiral (outlined in red and with a star), pass through a B bead on the large spiral (outlined in red), then into the next B bead on the small spiral, and finally into the next B bead on the large spiral.

Make a knot, weave the thread away from the knot, and cut the thread.

Repeat the step described above to join three small spirals to each of the eight large spirals. Set the remaining small spirals aside.

▶ Join the Large Component Halves

1 Use right angle weave to zip two halves of a large component together, leaving an opening about ¾ inch long to allow for stuffing the large spiral in the next step.

2 Stuff the large spiral component with Press'n Seal, then complete the zip.

Repeat steps 1 and 2 to make a total of four large three-dimensional components.

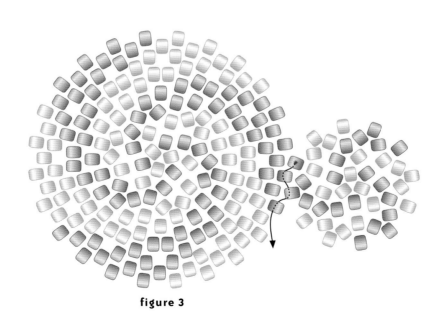

figure 3

▶ Central Focal Element

Refer to figure 4 for placement of the components for the focal element.

1 Zip two large components together by joining two top and two bottom small spirals with right angle weave.

2 With the thread exiting the lower bead of the top join, pick up one pearl, one 15°, one crystal, one 15°, and the remaining pearl. Pass through the upper bead of the bottom join. Repeat the thread path for added strength.

3 With the thread exiting a cylinder A bead to the right or left of the lowest join, pick up one cylinder A, one crystal, three cylinder As, three 15°s, the drop, three 15°s, and two cylinder As. Pass back through the cylinder A below the crystal, pick up one crystal and one cylinder A, and pass through the cylinder A opposite the one first exited. Repeat the thread path for added strength.

▶ Closure

The closure is made with two small spirals joined together to create a button that then fits into the center of a larger spiral made with a hole in the center.

Spiral Button

Zip two small spirals together with right angle weave. Set aside.

Spiral Toggle

Rows 1 and 2 Pick up four cylinder Bs, four cylinder As, four cylinder Bs, four cylinder As, four cylinder Bs, and four cylinder As, for a total of 24 beads. Pass through all the beads again to form a circle, then pass through the first B as shown in figure 5 (the first B is identified with a star).

Row 3 Continue with peyote stitch, following the color pattern in the diagram to begin to create the spiral. ***Tip:*** Pick up the same color bead as the one you've just *exited*. Step up through the first bead added.

Row 4 Work regular peyote following the color pattern in the diagram (picking up the same color bead as the one you've just exited). Step up through the first bead added.

Rows 5–9 Follow the instructions for rows 9 through 13 of Large Spiral, but pick up the same color of bead(s) as the bead(s) you've just exited.

Repeat rows 1 through 9 to make a second toggle spiral.

Assemble the Toggle

1 Follow the instructions for Large Component Halves to attach three small spirals to each of the toggle halves.

2 Zip the outer edges of the toggle halves together with right angle weave.

3 Stitch the beads around the center hole together—don't use right angle weave, just weave in and out of each half. Set the toggle aside.

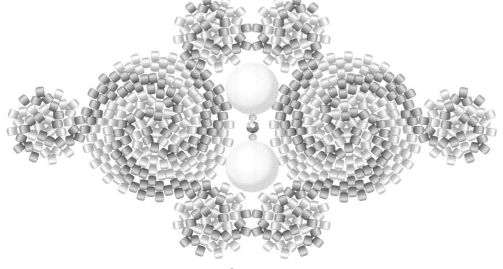

figure 4

figure 5

► Chain

To complete the necklace, you'll attach the components to sections of right angle weave chain made with size 11° round seed beads. All four sections of chain are four units across. Two of the sections are 15 units long and two sections are 58 units long. I use both metallic gold (A) and matte gold (C) so that the chain doesn't overpower the focal pieces.

1 Working right angle weave, follow the color pattern in figure 6 to make the four sections of chain sized as outlined above.

2 To curve the two short sections, weave through the beadwork to exit one of the beads on the edge of the chain, as shown in figure 6 (the bead is identified with a red star). *Pick up one C and pass through the first bead of the next right angle weave unit. Repeat from * three more times.

3 Pass through the next seven beads without adding any beads, forming the inner curve.

4 Repeat steps 2 and 3 to complete the other end. Pay particular attention to the tension of the piece—don't pull too tightly or the chain will warp. Tie a half-hitch knot to hold the curve in place.

5 For the outer curve, follow the pattern in figure 6 to add Cs and crystals.

► Assemble the Necklace

1 With the curve moving away from the center, use right angle weave to zip a short section of chain to the top of a large spiral of the center focal piece. Repeat on the other side.

2 Attach the other end of each of the shorter chains to a large component using the same method.

3 Attach one end of each of the longer chains to the top inside of the two large components.

4 Attach the spiral toggle to the other end of one long chain.

5 Attach the button (the remaining small spiral component) to the other end of the chain as follows: With the thread exiting the top bead of an outer right angle weave unit, *pick up one 11° C and pass through the top bead of the right angle unit. Repeat from * two more times, adding three beads total. Weave through the beadwork to exit toward the center through the last 11° C added. *Pick up one 11° A and pass through the next 11° C. Repeat from *, adding two beads total. Weave through the beadwork to exit toward the center through the last 11° A added. Pick up four cylinder As, pass through the first two beads again, then through the next 11° A. Weave through

The closure

the beadwork to exit the top of the four-bead unit just added. Pass through a bead on the small spiral component. Reinforce the join by passing through all four-bead units and the small spiral several times.

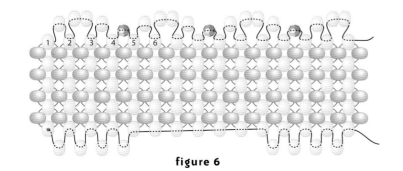

figure 6

LAKSMI PENDANT

Laksmi is the Hindu goddess of wealth, prosperity, light, wisdom, fortune, fertility, generosity, and courage; she's also the embodiment of beauty, grace, and charm. A carved ivory statuette of Laksmi was found in a house in Pompeii along with pearls and precious stones from India and records of the Nabatean cults. This pendant is based on that statuette and a photo of an amulet I found in a book about ancient Indian jewelry.

▶ End Caps

Refer to figure 1 for rows 1 through 14 of the center disc. All rows are worked with cylinder beads in color A.

Rows 1–6 Complete six rows of circular peyote stitch.

Rows 7 and 8 Complete two rows of regular peyote stitch, stepping up at the end of the row through the first bead added.

Row 9 *Pick up two beads and pass through the next bead in row 8. Repeat from * 11 more times, for a total of 12 sets of two beads. At the end of the row, step up through the first two beads added.

Row 10 *Pick up one bead and pass through the next two beads in row 9 (treating them as one). Repeat from * to add a total of 12 beads. At the end of the row, step up through the first bead added.

SUPPLIES

Basic Beading Kit (page 11)

Size 11° cylinder beads:

Color A, sterling silver plated matte metallic, approximately 15 g

Color B, sterling silver metallic, approximately 7 g

Size 15° sterling silver round seed beads, 10 g

52 black semiprecious or crystal beads, 2 mm

3 black semiprecious stones, 3 mm

1 black faceted drop, approximately 10 x 15 mm

1 coin pearl, 10 mm

1 strand of 3-mm glass pearls

FINISHED SIZE

Pendant, 2⅛ x 2½ inches (5.4 x 6.4 cm)

Chain, 19 inches (48.3 cm) long

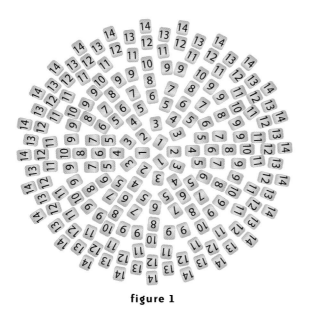

figure 1

Row 11 *Pick up two beads and pass through the next bead in row 10. Repeat from * to add a total of 12 sets of two beads. At the end of the row, step up through the first bead added, splitting the pair.

Row 12 *Pick up one bead and pass through the second bead of the pair. Pick up one bead and pass through the first bead of the next pair. Repeat from * to add a total of 24 beads. At the end of the row, step up through the first bead added.

Rows 13 and 14 Work two rows of regular peyote stitch.

When row 14 is completed, set the piece aside and repeat rows 1 through 14 to make another disc with color A. Zip the two pieces together.

Repeat all instructions again to make a second end cap.

Build Up the End Points

In this step, you'll work with color B on one side of each of the double discs just created.

Row 1 With the thread exiting a bead on row 8 on one side of a disc as shown in figure 2, *pick up two beads and pass through the next bead in the row. Repeat from * to complete the row. Step up through the first two beads added (treat two beads as one).

Row 2 *Pick up one bead and pass through the next two beads in row 1. Repeat from * to complete the row. Step up through the first bead added.

Row 3 Pick up two beads and pass through the next bead in row 2. Repeat from * to complete the row. Step up through the first two beads added.

Row 4 *Pick up one bead and pass through the next two beads in row 3. Repeat from * to complete the row. Step up through the first bead added.

Row 5 *Pick up one bead and pass through the next up bead in the previous row. Repeat from * to complete the row.

Rows 6–9 Work four rows with regular peyote stitch, stepping up at the end of each row through the first bead added in that row.

Row 10 This is a decrease row. *Pick up one bead and pass through the next up bead, the next down bead, and then the next up bead. Repeat from * to complete the row. Step up through the first bead added.

Row 11 Pick up two beads and pass through the next up bead. Repeat so there are two beads in each decrease spot. Step up at the end of the row through the first two beads added.

Row 12 *Pick up one bead and pass through the next two beads. Repeat from * to complete the row. Step up through the first bead added.

Row 13 *Pick up one bead and pass through the next up bead in the previous row. Repeat from * to complete the row. Close up the top by passing through all the beads added in this row.

Repeat rows 1 through 13 on the second end cap.

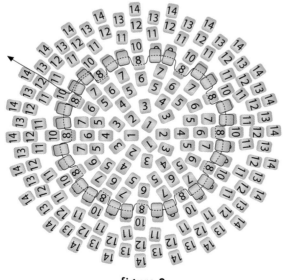

figure 2

Setup for the Tube

In this step you'll work with color B on the other end of each of the double discs, which now have one end built up.

Row 1 With the thread exiting a bead in row 8 on the other side of the disc (refer to figure 2 for the row setup), add two beads in each spot as you did for the top of the piece.

Row 2 *Pick up one bead and pass through the next two beads in row 1. Repeat from * to complete the row. Step up through the first bead added.

Row 3 *Pick up two beads and pass through the next bead in row 2. Repeat from * to complete the row. Step up through the first bead added, splitting the pair.

Row 4 *Pick up one bead and pass through the second bead of the pair. Pick up one bead and pass through the first bead of the next pair. Repeat from * to complete the row. At the end of the row, step up through the first bead added.

Rows 5–8 Work four rows with regular peyote stitch.

Row 9 This is a decrease row. *Pick up one bead and pass through the next up bead, the next down bead, and then the next up bead. Repeat from * to complete the row.

Row 10 Pick up two beads and pass through the next up bead. Repeat so there are two beads in each decrease spot. Step up at the end of the row through the first two beads added.

Repeat rows 1 through 10 for the other end cap.

▶ Tube

1 With the thread exiting a bead in row 10, which was just completed, and working with color A, *pick up one bead and pass through the next two beads. Repeat from * to complete the row. Step up through the first bead added.

2 Pick up two beads and pass through the next bead. Repeat from * to complete the row. Step up through the first two beads added.

3 Repeat these two rows until 27 rows are completed. The last row will be like the first: pick up one bead and pass through two beads.

4 Zip the tube to row 10 of the other end cap.

▶ Bail

The bail is made with two-drop peyote stitch consisting of eight sets of two beads in color A.

1 String on a stopper bead, then string on 16 beads. *Pick up two beads and make a flat peyote turn, skipping the first two beads and passing through the next set of two beads as shown in figure 3. Repeat from * to complete the row (figure 4).

2 At the end of the row, pick up two beads and make a flat peyote turn as shown in figure 5. Continue for about 36 rows and zip the two ends together to form a tube that will fit around your chain. Attach the bail to the tubular part of the component.

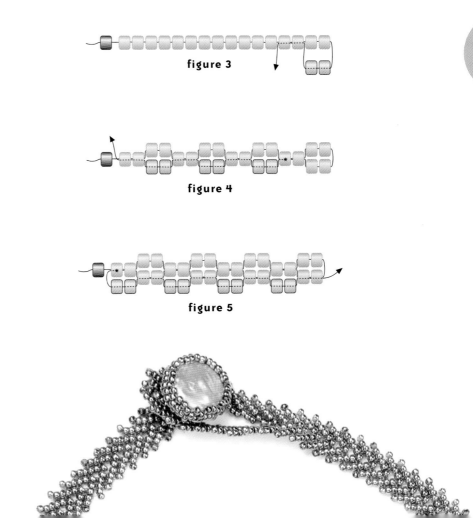

figure 3

figure 4

figure 5

► Embellish

You'll embellish the tube with 15° round seed beads, 2-mm semiprecious or crystal beads, and 3-mm crystals around the end caps and along the join to the bail. Refer to figure 6 for placement.

With a simple color change, the Laksmi design takes on a completely different look.

1 With the thread exiting a bead in row 9 on one end cap where the tube begins, *pick up three size 15°s and pass through the next bead in row 9. Repeat from * to complete the row.

2 Move to the seam between the two discs and stitch in the ditch with one 15°, one 2-mm bead, and one 15° for the entire row.

3 With the thread exiting row 9 on the outer disc where the built-up end begins, repeat step 2.

4 Embellish the seam where the bail meets the tube with a pattern of two 15°s, one 3-mm stone, three 15°s, one 3-mm stone, three 15°s, one 3-mm stone, and two 15°s.

5 To make a peyote stitch tube of 15°s, pick up eight beads and pass through them again to form a circle. Step up through the first bead added. Work even-count tubular peyote stitch until the tube is 1¹⁄₁₆ inches (2.7 cm) long. Repeat to make a second tube. Attach one end of

a tube to the bottom of each outer disc of the end cap, and the other end to the center of the component.

6 Add the drop with a loop of 15°s.

► Chain

The chain is a double St. Petersburg made with 15°s, and the closure is a bezeled coin pearl with two lengths of single St. Petersburg chain joined together to make a loop.

Use 15°s for all steps.

Refer to figure 7 for steps 1 through 3.

1 String on a stopper bead, pick up six squares, and pass through the third and fourth bead.

2 Pick up one 15° and pass back down through three squares.

3 Pick up one glass pearl and pass through the fifth and sixth square beads.

Continue with St. Petersburg chain to the length required.

4 To double the chain, start a new thread and repeat steps 1 and 2. Pass through the glass pearl on the first chain and through the two squares as shown in figure 8. *Pick up four squares and pass through the first and second beads. Pick up one 15° and pass back through three squares. Pass through the pearl and two squares. Continue from * until the chain is completed (figure 9).

5 At one end of the chain, make two lengths of single St. Petersburg chain to fit around the bezeled pearl and ladder stitch them together to form a loop.

6 Attach the bezeled pearl to the other end of the chain.

7 Slide the chain through the bail.

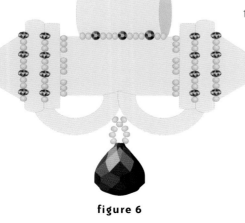

figure 6

figure 7

figure 8

figure 9

SUPPLIES

Basic Beading Kit (page 11)

Size 11° gold matte metallic cylinder beads, < 1 g

Size 15° round seed beads:

Color A, gold metallic, < 1 g

Color B, emerald green, 8 beads

Size 10° gold matte metallic cylinder beads, < 1 g

4 faceted garnet nailheads, 6 mm

8 metallic gold drop beads, 3.4 mm

8 emerald faceted beads, 2 mm

6 opal drops with side-drilled hole, 5 x 10 mm

2 gold-filled lever-back ear wires

FINISHED SIZE

2½ inches (6.4 cm) long

ZOE

Empress Zoe reigned over the Byzantine Empire during the eleventh century. Her image was captured in a mosaic located in the Hagia Sophia in Istanbul, and these earrings are inspired by the pair depicted there. Each earring is made with two squares—each with differently sized beads. They are joined together and embellished with garnets, small drops, and seed beads.

Row 2 Pick up one bead and pass through the next bead in row 1. Repeat three more times for a total of four beads for the row. Step up through the first bead added in the row.

Row 3 Pick up two beads and pass through the next bead in row 2. Repeat three more times for a total of eight beads (four sets of two) for the row. Step up through the first bead added, splitting the pair.

Row 4 *Pick up one bead and pass through the second bead in the pair. Pick up one bead and pass through the first bead of the next pair in row 3. Repeat from * three more times for a total of eight beads in the row. Step up through the first bead added.

Row 5 This is where the setup for the square shape begins. *Pick up two beads and pass through the next bead in row 4, then pick up one bead and pass through the next bead in row 4. Repeat from * to complete the row. Step up through the first two beads added in the row.

Row 6 Continue with a row of singular peyote, picking up one bead and passing through the next bead, then picking up one bead and passing through the next two beads, treating the two beads as one.

Step up through the first bead added in the row.

Row 7 *Pick up one bead and pass through the next bead in row 6; pick up four beads and pass through the next bead in row 6. Repeat from * three times to complete the row. Step up through the first bead added in this row.

Row 8 *Weave over to the four-bead corner and pass through the first two corner beads; pick up one bead and pass through the next two corner beads. Repeat from * to complete three more corners.

Embellish the Small Square

Row 1 With the thread exiting a bead in row 1, pick up a garnet nailhead and pass through the bead in row 1 that is directly across from the bead exited, then pass back through the garnet and the original bead exited. Step up into a bead in row 2.

Row 2 *Pick up three 15° As and pass through the next bead in row 2. Repeat from * to complete the row and step up through the first three beads added.

Row 3 *Pick up two 15° As and pass through the next three beads added in row 2. Repeat from * to complete the row and step up through the first two beads added (figure 2).

▶ Small Square

The smaller top square is made with circular peyote stitch using size 11° cylinder beads. Rows 1 through 8 are illustrated in figure 1. Cylinder beads are used throughout, and the red outlined beads indicate the first bead and the step up at the end of each row.

Row 1 Pick up four cylinder beads and pass through them again to form a circle. Step up through the first bead strung.

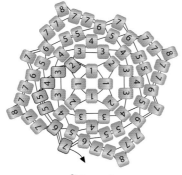

figure 1

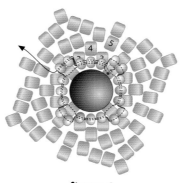

figure 2

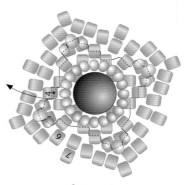

figure 3

Rows 4 and 5 Working off the ring formed in rows 2 and 3, work two rows of regular peyote stitch around the garnet.

Row 6 To secure the garnet, *pick up one 15° A and pass through the next up bead in the row. Complete a gradual decrease in the next peyote spot by passing down through the next bead in row 4 and back up through the next bead in row 5. Repeat from * to complete the row.

Row 7 Weave back down to the base and exit a bead in one of the corners of base row 4. Pick up one 15° A, one 15° B, and one 15° A; pass through the next bead in the base row 4 corner. The picot should sit in the corner of the square. Weave to the next corner of the square and repeat, then repeat again in the remaining two corners (figure 3).

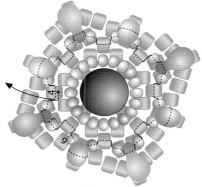

figure 4

▶ Large Square

Repeat the instructions for the small square, but make the piece using size 10° cylinder beads.

Embellish the Large Square

Rows 1–6 Repeat rows 1 through 6 of Embellish the Small Square to place and anchor a garnet.

Row 7 Weave back down to the base and exit a bead in one of the corners of base row 4. *Pick up one 15° A, one gold drop bead, and one 15° A; pass through the next bead in base row 4 so the drop lies in the corner. Pick up one 15° A, one faceted emerald, and one 15° A; pass through the next bead in row 4. Repeat from * to complete the row (figure 4).

▶ Join the Squares

Position two squares as shown in figure 5. With the thread exiting one of the beads on the smaller square, pick up one 11° cylinder bead and pass through the corresponding bead on the larger square, and then pick up one 11° cylinder and pass back through the bead on the smaller square. Continue with right angle weave, joining the rest of the beads shown in figure 5.

▶ Final Touches

Refer to figure 6 for steps 1 and 2.

1 Add the opal drops with 15° As, as shown in the illustration.

2 With the thread exiting a bead on the top of the smaller square, pick up three 15° As, pass through the hole on the ear wire, pick up three more 15° As, and pass through another bead on the square as shown. Repeat the thread path to reinforce.

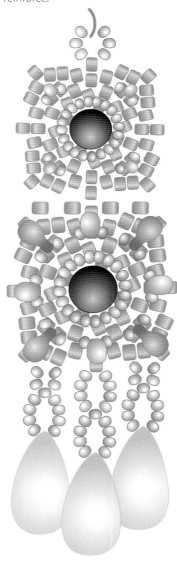

figure 6

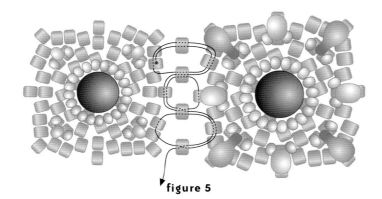

figure 5

CHAPTER FOUR
MOSAIC & TEXTILE MOTIFS AS INSPIRATION

After a museum visit gave me the idea of reinterpreting the jewelry of antiquity with seed beads, I began to look differently at everything, from ancient tilework to the pavement on the streets. And perhaps more than any other medium, mosaic and rug patterns lend themselves wonderfully to translation with beads.

If you think of tesserae—small tiles made of stone and glass—as beads, the motifs and lines of a mosaic design can most definitely be captured with seed beads, and especially cylinder beads.

The rug patterns of Turkey and the Middle East also lend themselves to being reimagined using beads instead of fibers. Brick stitch and peyote are wonderful stitches for doing pattern work, and the current bead colors available perfectly capture the look of the tapestries. As you'll see with the project called Solomon's Knot, right angle weave is great for building mosaic knots and braids that have been adapted into three-dimensional designs.

ANATOLIA

I'm fascinated by the kilim carpets made in the Anatolian region of Turkey. Village women of the region weave the kilims and their symbols, which represent phases of life and vary from village to village. This necklace uses motifs and colors found in these kilims.

► Cross Motifs

The center of the cross motif uses a circular peyote stitch started with color A cylinder beads. You'll make the arms with a variation of flat peyote stitch, using color B cylinder beads outlined with color A.

1 Pick up four cylinder As and pass through them again to form a circle. Step up through the first bead.

2 Pick up one cylinder A and pass through the next bead in the circle. Repeat to add one bead between each of the beads in row 1. Step up through the first bead added in this row.

3 Pick up two cylinder As and pass through the next bead in row 2. Repeat to add two beads between each of the beads in row 2. Step up through the first bead added in this row, splitting the pair

(figure 1, beads 1 and 2). You're now in position to begin one of the arms of the cross.

4 Pick up one cylinder B (figure 2, bead 3) and pass through the next cylinder A (figure 2, bead 2). Pick up one cylinder A (figure 2, bead 4) and pass through the cylinder B just added (figure 2, bead 3).

5 Make a figure-eight odd-count peyote turn as follows. Pick up one cylinder A (figure 3, bead 5), and pass through beads 1, 3, 2, and 4. Complete the figure eight by passing back through beads 3, 1, and 5. You're in position to add the next set of beads.

6 Pick up two cylinder Bs (figure 4, beads 6 and 7) and pass through the next cylinder A (bead 4). Pick up one cylinder A (figure 4, bead 8, on page 66) and pass back through beads 7 and 6.

SUPPLIES

Basic Beading Kit (page 11)

Size 11° cylinder beads:

    Color A, antiqued gold, approximately 7 g

    Color B, turquoise, approximately 4 g

    Color C, red brick, approximately 7 g

3 button-style pearls, 8 mm

90 semiprecious stones, 2 mm

Size 8° hex cut beads to match color C, 20 g

1 gold bead, 6 mm

1 turquoise faceted drop, 6 x 9 mm

1 gold 3-strand tube clasp

FINISHED SIZE

23 inches (58.4 cm) long

figure 1

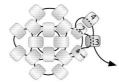

figure 2

figure 3

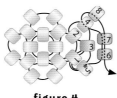

figure 4

figure 5

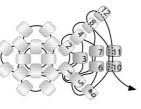

figure 6

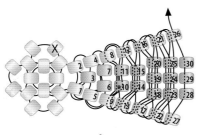

figure 7

7 Pick up one cylinder A (figure 5, bead 9) and pass through beads 5, 6, 7, 4, and 8. Pass back through beads 7, 6, and 5, and then back through the first bead added, bead 9.

8 With the thread exiting bead 9, pick up two cylinder Bs (figure 6, beads 10 and 11) and pass through bead 8. With the thread exiting bead 8, pick up one cylinder A (bead 12) and pass through beads 11 and 10.

9 Refer to figure 7 for the remaining rows. With the thread exiting bead 10, pick up one cylinder A (bead 13) and pass through beads 9, 10, 11, 8, and 12. To complete the figure-eight turn, pass back through beads 11, 10, and 9, and the first bead added, bead 13.

10 With the thread exiting bead 13, pick up two cylinder Bs (beads 14 and 15) and pass through bead 12. Pick up one cylinder A (bead 16) and pass through beads 15 and 14.

11 With the thread exiting bead 14, pick up one cylinder A (bead 17) and make the figure-eight turn through beads 13, 14, 15, 12, and 16, then back through 15, 14, 13, and 17.

12 Pick up three cylinder Bs (beads 18, 19, and 20) and pass through bead 16. Pick up one cylinder A (bead 21) and pass back through beads 20, 19, and 18.

13 With the thread exiting bead 18, pick up one cylinder A (bead 22) and make the figure-eight turn as before, exiting bead 22. Pick up three cylinder Bs (beads 23, 24, and 25) and pass through bead 21. Pick up one cylinder A (bead 26) and go back through beads 25, 24, and 23.

14 To make the last figure-eight turn for this arm, pick up one cylinder A (bead 27)

and make the figure-eight turn to exit the same bead, bead 27. Pick up three cylinder Bs (beads 28, 29, and 30) and pass through bead 26.

15 Weave through to the starting point for the next arm (marked with an X in figure 7) and repeat steps 1 through 14. Complete the remaining two arms for the cross shape. Tie off the thread.

Repeat steps 1 through 15 to make a total of 12 cross pieces.

Join the Cross Motifs

The crosses are joined together with right angle weave at the points outlined in red in figure 8.

1 With the needle exiting an ending edge bead, pick up one cylinder A and pass through an ending edge bead on the next cross. Pick up one cylinder A and pass through the first bead exited.

2 Repeat step 1 at all points of four crosses as shown in figure 8.

3 Using cylinder As, bezel a button pearl as you would bezel a coin pearl, but attach the pearl at the completion of row 4 instead of row 6, and then continue with peyote stitch to capture the pearl. Place the component in the center of the cross motif and attach the bezels to the ending beads of the crosses.

4 In the centers of the small crosses, attach the small semiprecious stones using a figure-eight anchor.

Repeat steps 1 through 4 with the remaining small crosses to create two more large motifs.

figure 8

▶ Triangle Motifs

The second pattern is made with separate flat brick stitch triangles that you then stitch together to form the motifs.

Small Triangles

1 Make a bead ladder of seven cylinder As.

2 Working brick stitch, pick up one cylinder A and one cylinder C and pass under the second connecting thread and up through the cylinder C. Complete the row following the color pattern in figure 9.

3 Following the color pattern in figure 9, work four more rows of regular flat brick stitch for a total of six rows.

Repeat steps 1 through 3 to make a total of 16 small triangles.

Large Triangles

1 With cylinder A, make a base row of nine beads.

2 Continuing with flat brick stitch as for the small triangles, follow the color pattern in figure 10 for a total of eight rows.

Repeat steps 1 and 2 to make a total of eight large triangles.

Join the Triangles

1 Position two small triangles so the top two beads of each triangle line up. With the thread exiting one of the top beads of the first triangle, pass through the corresponding bead of the second triangle. The beads to be joined are outlined in red in figure 11.

2 Pass through the second top bead of the second triangle, then through the corresponding bead of the first triangle. Repeat the thread path to strengthen the join.

Repeat steps 1 and 2 to join two more small triangles.

3 Position the four triangles side by side as shown in figure 11 and join the edge beads on the base rows together.

4 Attach two large triangles, one on the top of the component and one on the bottom, as shown in figure 12.

Repeat steps 1 through 4 to make a total of four components.

figure 9

figure 10

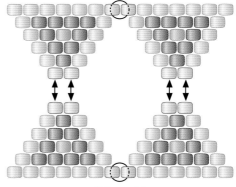

figure 11

► Diagonal Motifs

The third motif comprises components made with diagonal and flat brick stitch.

1 Make a bead ladder of one cylinder A and seven cylinder Cs. Following the color pattern in figure 13, work in diagonal brick stitch to complete five rows.

Repeat step 1 to make a total of eight diagonal brick stitch components.

2 Make a bead ladder of one cylinder A, 14 cylinder Cs, and one cylinder A. Using brick stitch, follow the color pattern in figure 14 to complete five rows.

Repeat step 2 to make a total of two flat brick stitch components.

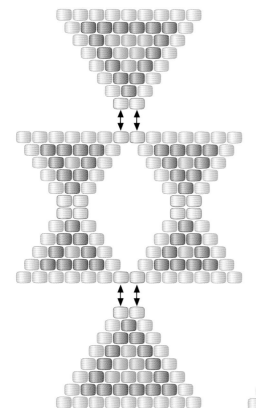

figure 12

figure 13

figure 14

3 Stitch the pieces together as shown in figure 15, matching the three beads on one component to three beads on the other component.

Repeat steps 1 through 3 to make a second component.

► **Final Assembly**

1 Referring to the photo for placement, join the seven large components together with single right angle weave units, as was done with the smaller crosses, using 2-mm semiprecious stones.

2 Make two right angle weave straps with cylinder As and size 8° hex cut beads. Each strap should be five units wide and 4¼ inches (11.4 cm) long. For the first unit, pick up one cylinder A, one 8° hex, one cylinder A, and one 8° hex.

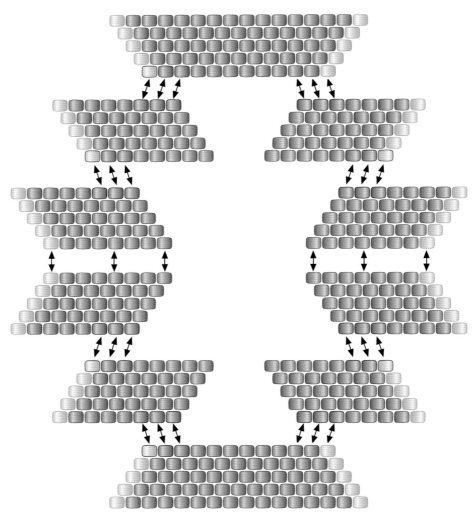

figure 15

The back and closure

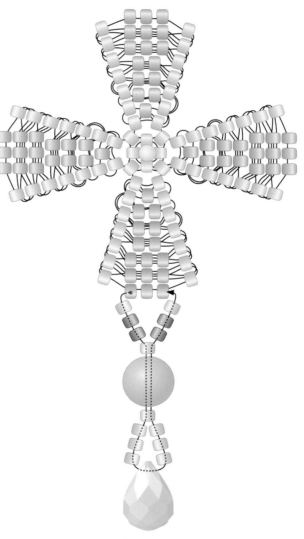

3 Attach one strap to each side of the necklace with single right angle weave units and semiprecious stones.

4 Attach the drop to the center cross piece of the necklace. With the thread exiting one side of the bottom arm of the cross, pick up one cylinder A, one cylinder C, one cylinder A, the 6-mm gold bead, four cylinder As, the drop, and three cylinder As; pass through one cylinder A, the gold bead, and one cylinder A; pick up one cylinder C, and one cylinder A; pass through the three bottoms beads on the cross (figure 16).

5 Attach the ends of the right angle weave straps to the three-strand tube clasp and embellish with the semiprecious stones.

figure 16

SOLOMON'S KNOT PENDANT

The Solomon's Knot motif appears in many different cultures and in different mediums, such as mosaics and embroidery. Books and symposiums have been devoted to this motif alone. The pendant is made using right angle weave following a color pattern. You'll make two ovals, each with a different inside color, and braid them together to form the knot.

▶ Ovals

1 Using cylinder A and B beads, make two right angle weave pieces seven units wide and 10 units long, following the color pattern in figure 1.

2 Fold the piece in half as shown in figure 2 so you have a border of cylinder A beads on each side. Using more cylinder A beads, zip the open side as shown in figure 3. When zipping up a piece, you're completing right angle weave units by adding a bead between two other units.

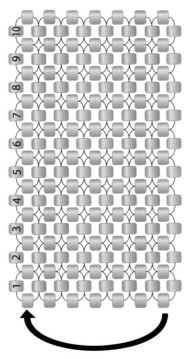

figure 2

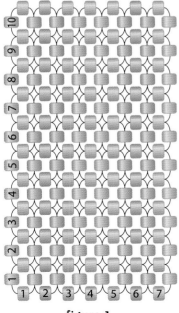

figure 1

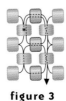

figure 3

SUPPLIES

Basic Beading Kit (page 11)

Size 11° cylinder beads:

  Color A, antiqued gold, 12 g

  Color B, matte olive, 4 g

  Color C, burgundy, 4 g

1 burgundy pearl drop bead, 10 x 12 mm

8 dark olive Swarovski glass pearls, 5 mm

2 burgundy Swarovski glass pearls, 6 mm

1 gold button-style pearl, 8–10 mm

6 burgundy drop beads, 3.4 mm

FINISHED SIZE

Pendant, 3½ x 1⅞ inches (8.9 x 4.7 cm)

Chain, 19 inches (48.3 cm) long

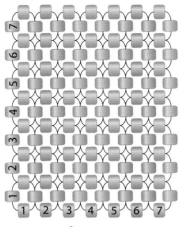

figure 4

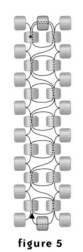

figure 5

3 Make two more pieces of right angle weave, seven units wide and seven units long following the same color pattern (figure 4). These pieces will become the curves of the oval.

4 Fold the shorter pieces in half lengthwise and ladder stitch the open sides together. The ladder stitch pulls the beads in, and these pieces will form the curves of the oval. Add one bead on each end (the beads are outlined in red in figure 5). These two beads are added for joining with the right angle weave side pieces.

5 With the thread exiting an edge bead on one side (figure 6), pass through all of the beads on this side of the piece and pull taut, causing the piece to curve. Weave through the beadwork and pass through the corresponding beads on the other side to complete the curve. Pull the thread taut and make a half-hitch knot to hold the curve in place.

6 Repeat steps 1 through 5 with colors A and C to form the pieces for the second oval.

You'll now join the pieces of the first oval with a series of increases.

1 Place one side piece and one curved piece together as shown in figure 7.

Refer to figure 8 for steps 2 through 7.

2 With the thread exiting a bead on the straight piece, as identified by a star in the illustration, pick up one cylinder A and pass through the corresponding bead on the curved piece.

3 Pick up one cylinder B (bead 2 in the illustration) and pass through the first bead exited, the next two As, the bead just added, and the end bead of the middle unit on the straight piece. Pick up two Bs (beads 3 and 4), and pass through the corresponding bead on the curved piece, bead 2, the first bead exited in this step, and the first of the two beads added (bead 3), splitting the pair.

4 Pick up two As (beads 5 and 6) and make a right angle weave unit, passing through the end bead of the straight piece, bead 3, and bead 5.

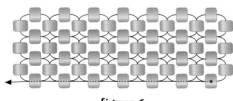

figure 6

figure 7

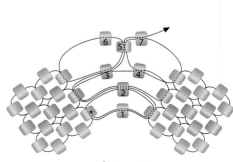

figure 8

74

5 Pick up one A (bead 7) and make another right angle weave unit by passing through the corresponding end bead of the curved piece, beads 4 and 5, and again through the bead just added.

6 To complete the join on the other side, weave back down to bead 1 and repeat steps 2 through 5.

7 Repeat steps 1 through 6 to make the second half of the oval. Join the two halves together in both places, again following steps 1 through 6.

Join the Second Oval

Follow steps 1 through 7 of Join the First Oval with cylinder Cs for the pieces of the second oval, but join the two halves together in one place only, leaving an opening in the oval.

▶ Complete the Knot

Refer to figure 9 for the next two steps.

1 Braid the two ovals together as shown. Complete the final join as outlined above to complete the knot.

2 Tack the knot down at the four points shown by passing through beads on both pieces so the thread doesn't show. The two ovals become one solid piece.

Complete the Pendant

1 Embellish the inner and outer edges of the knot by stitching in the ditch with cylinder As, as shown in figure 10.

2 With the thread exiting a bead slightly to the right of bottom center, pick up six As, the large drop pearl, and one A; pass back through the pearl and one A bead; pick up five As and pass through the corresponding bead to the left of bottom center. Repeat the thread path several times to reinforce.

▶ Bail

Make a tubular herringbone bail to attach the knot to a chain, as follows:

1 Make a bead ladder with 16 cylinder As.

2 Using cylinder Cs, complete three rows of tubular herringbone stitch.

3 Complete one row of tubular herringbone with As.

4 Complete three more rows of tubular herringbone with Cs.

5 Complete the last row of tubular herringbone with As.

6 Center the bail on top of the knot and ladder stitch the pieces together with A.

▶ Chain

The chain for the pendant is made of three sections of tubular herringbone stitch—two long pieces and one short piece.

Long Tubes

1 Make a bead ladder of eight beads with cylinder As.

2 Complete 18 rows of tubular herringbone with As.

3 Complete three rows of tubular herringbone with Bs.

4 Complete one row of tubular herringbone with As.

5 Complete three rows of tubular herringbone with Bs.

6 Complete 19 rows of tubular herringbone with As.

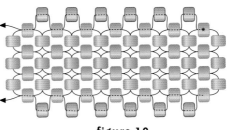

figure 9

figure 10

The ovals used in this necklace are very versatile. You can make a pair to dangle from ear wires, for example, or connect three of them to make a bracelet, as shown here.

7 Repeat steps 3 through 5, but this time with Cs.

8 Complete 19 rows of tubular herringbone with As.

9 Repeat steps 3 through 6.

10 Set the tube aside and make another tube following steps 1 through 9.

Short Tube

This tube will hold the pendant.

1 Make a bead ladder of eight beads with As.

2 Complete 18 rows of tubular herringbone with As.

3 Complete three rows of tubular herringbone with Bs.

4 Complete one row of tubular herringbone with As.

5 Complete three rows of tubular herringbone with Bs.

6 Complete 19 rows of tubular herringbone with As.

7 Repeat steps 3 through 6.

▶ Complete the Chain

1 Thread the short tube through the bale on the pendant.

2 With the thread exiting a bead on one end of the short tube, string two 5-mm pearls, one 6-mm pearl, and two 5-mm pearls.

3 Pass through a bead on one end of a long tube, anchor the thread through several beads on the tube, pass back through the strand of pearls, and anchor the thread through several beads on the end of the short tube. Make sure the strand is centered neatly over the holes of the tubes.

4 Repeat steps 1 through 3 for the other side of the chain.

5 Taper the ends of the chain as follows. *With the thread exiting an end bead, pick up two cylinder As. Skip the next end bead and pass through the following bead. Repeat from * to add four columns of two beads evenly spaced. With the thread exiting an end bead on one column, pick up one A and pass through the two beads of the next column. Catch a thread and pass back through the two beads of the column and the ending A. Repeat on all columns to join them together through the one end bead.

▶ Closure

1 Bezel the button pearl with cylinder As. Embellish the sides of the bezel with two picots made of three small drop beads each.

2 With the thread exiting a bead in row 2 of the bezel, pick up two As, pass through the end bead on one end of the chain, pick up two As, and pass through the corresponding bead in row 2 of the bezel. Repeat the thread path several times to reinforce.

3 To make a loop closure to fit over the pearl, string the number of cylinder beads required to form a loop that allows the bezeled pearl to pass through. Secure the loop and then work one row of peyote stitch—this is not only decorative but also gives the loop strength.

MOROCCAN TILE BROOCH

I own a tile from Morocco, and its pattern just seemed a natural for a brooch. The piece is made of small pieces of flat brick stitch that are then joined in puzzle fashion to create the pattern.

SUPPLIES

Basic Beading Kit (page 11)

Size 11° cylinder beads:

    Color A, antique gold metallic, 4 g

    Color B, Montana blue matte metallic, 4 g

Size 15° round beads:

    Color C, bronze, 2 g

    Color D, Montana blue metallic, 2 g

    24-karat gold plated, < 1 g

1 blue coin pearl, 10 mm

18 rice pearls, 3 mm

18 Montana blue crystals, 2 mm

1 pin back, 1³/₁₆ x ⁷/₁₆ inch (3 x 1.1 cm)

FINISHED SIZE

3 inches (7.6 cm) across

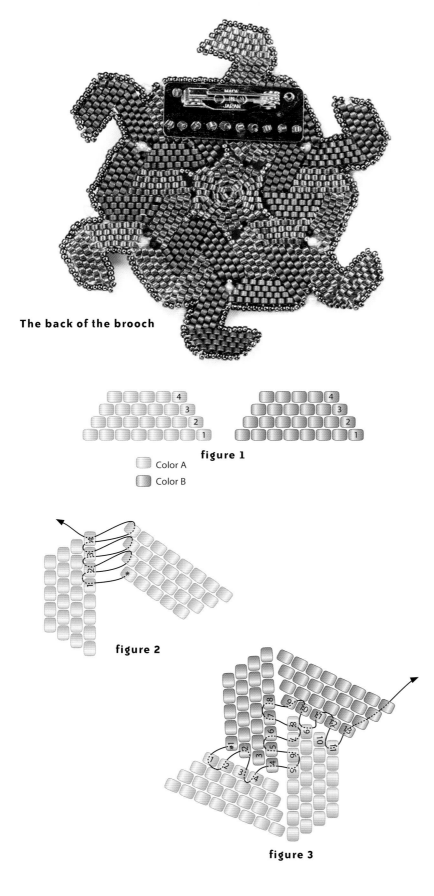

The back of the brooch

figure 1

Color A
Color B

figure 2

figure 3

► **Components**

1 Using cylinder As, make a bead ladder of eight beads and complete three more rows of flat brick stitch as shown in figure 1. Repeat to make 18 pieces total.

2 Repeat step 1 to make 18 pieces using cylinder Bs.

3 Position two pieces of the same color as shown in figure 2.

4 With the thread exiting bead 1 of the right-hand piece, pass through bead 1 of the left-hand piece. Pass through bead 2 of the left piece, then into bead 2 of the right piece.

5 Pass through bead 2 of the left piece again, then into bead 3 of the left piece.

6 Pass through bead 3 of the right piece, back through bead 3 of the left piece, and then through bead 4 of the left piece.

7 To complete the join, pass through bead 4 of the right piece and back into bead 4 of the left piece. Save the threads, if they're long enough, to use for connecting other components.

Repeat steps 1 through 7 to join the remaining 16 pieces of color A in sets of two, for a total of nine components. Repeat steps 1 through 7 to join 18 pieces of color B to make nine components.

► **Join the Components**

You'll create the "tile" by stitching the components together in a method similar to the one above for joining pieces.

1 Position one A component and one B component as shown in figure 3. With the thread exiting bead 1 in the B component, pass through bead 1 in the A component, bead 2 in the A component, and then bead 2 in the B component. Pass through bead 3 in the A component, bead 3 in the B component, bead 4 in the A component, and then bead 4 in the B component.

2 Follow the thread path shown in figure 3 as follows:

From bead 4 of B through bead 5 of A, then through bead 6 of A.

From bead 6 of A through bead 5 of B, then through bead 6 of B.

From bead 6 of B through bead 7 of A, then through bead 8 of A.

From bead 8 of A through bead 7 of B, then through bead 8 of B.

From bead 8 of B through bead 9 of B, then through bead 10 of B.

From bead 10 of B through bead 9 of A.

From bead 9 of A through bead 11 of B, then through bead 12 of B.

From bead 12 of B through bead 11 of A, then through bead 13 of A. Once again, leave the thread uncut to join components later.

Complete steps 1 and 2 five more times to make a total of six double components. The remaining six single components will be attached later to complete the pattern.

Complete the Join

1 Using a thread path as established above, join three double components together, then add two single components as shown in figure 4.

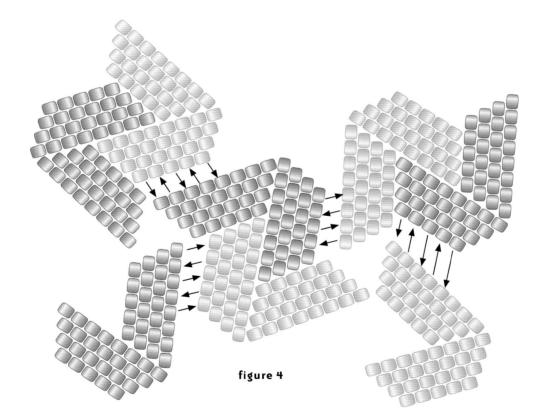

figure 4

2 Referring to figure 5, add the remaining double and single components to complete the tile. **Note**: There will be a hole in the center of the piece where you'll place a bezeled coin pearl in the next step.

▶ Embellish

1 Bezel the coin pearl with cylinder As.

2 Again referring to figure 5, place the bezeled pearl in the center of the tile. With the thread exiting row 9 of the bezel, pick up one gold 15°, one 15° D, and one gold 15°, and pass through a bead in the beadwork. Pass back through the three 15°s, and back into the bead in row 9 of the bezel. Repeat five more times at the points to securely attach the pearl to the beadwork.

3 Embellish around the bezel by stitching in the peyote ditch: *Pick up one 15° gold, one pearl, and one 15° gold, and pass through the next bead of the row. Pick up one 15° gold, one crystal, and one 15° gold, and then pass through the next bead of the row. Repeat from * five more times to complete the row.

4 Embellish the centers of the "pinwheel motif" with one 15° gold, one pearl, and one 15° gold, then add one crystal on each side of the pearl to fill the hole.

5 Referring to figure 5 for placement, add the remaining six rice pearls at the points on the outside of the pattern.

6 Backstitch around the outer edges with 15°s, in a pattern of one C followed by two Ds.

▶ Attach the Pin Back

Turn the piece over and place the pin back face down onto the beadwork, somewhere near an edge. Stitch the finding to the beadwork.

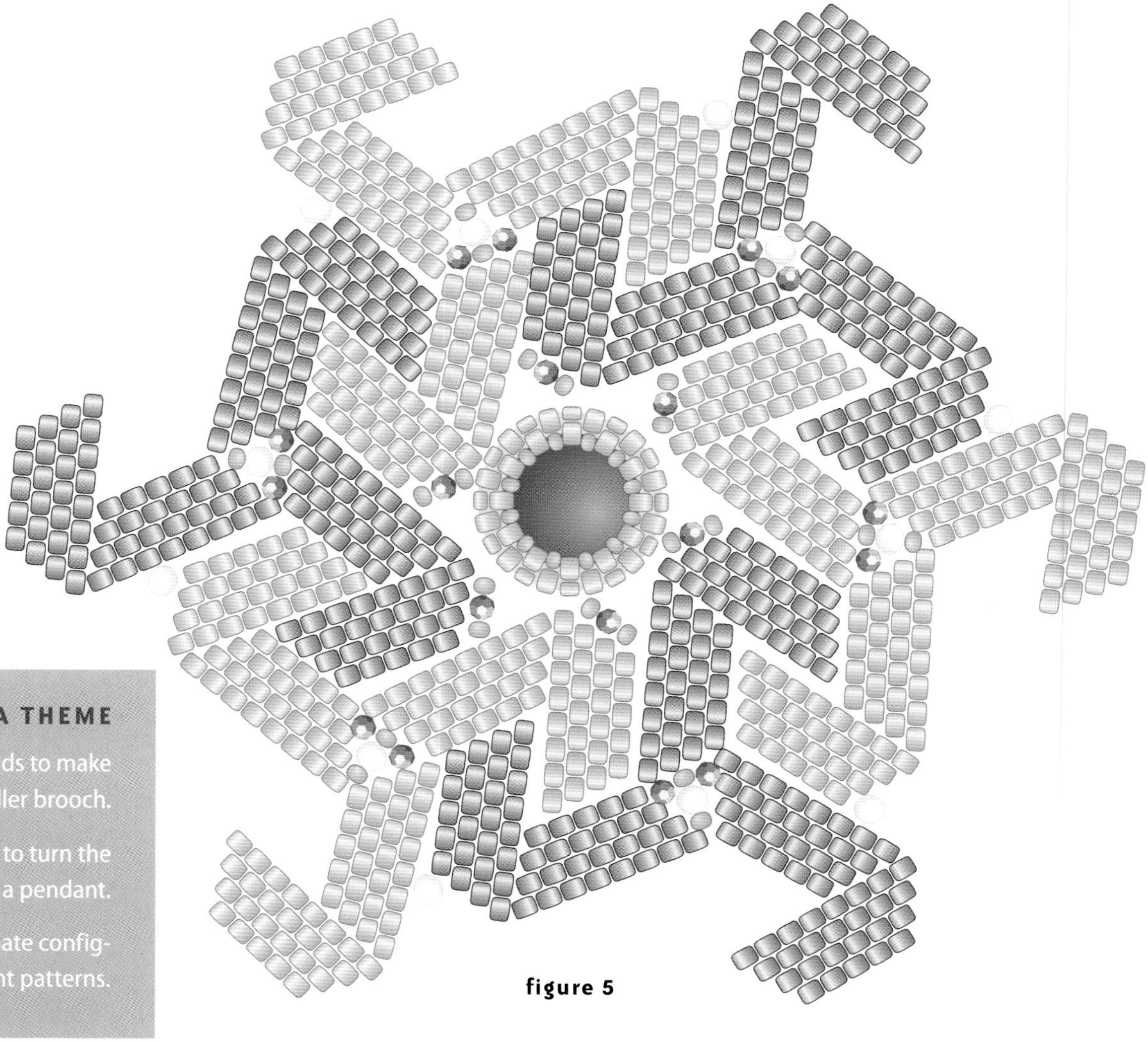

VARIATION ON A THEME

• Use size 15° cylinder beads to make a smaller brooch.

• Use a pin converter to turn the brooch into a pendant.

• Place the pieces in alternate configurations to make different patterns.

figure 5

TUCCIA

The flamelike pattern of fabric found in the Bargello Palace in Florence, popular in many needle arts, inspired these earrings. They're named after one of the Vestal Virgins from ancient Rome. The priestesses of the goddess Vesta were responsible for maintaining the sacred fire of the temple. Selected from distinguished families at an early age, they enjoyed privileges not permitted to other Roman women.

SUPPLIES

Basic Beading Kit (page 11)

Size 11° cylinder beads:

    Color A, medium blue, 2 g

    Color B, matte metallic gold, 2 g

    Color C, shiny sapphire, 2 g

2 golden coin pearls, 10 mm

Size 15° gold charlottes, 1 g

2 blue faceted glass side-drilled drops, 6 x 9 mm

2 gold lever-back ear wires

FINISHED SIZE

3⅛ inches (7.9 cm) long

OVERVIEW

The positioning of rows and the placement of colors creates the flamelike pattern. Each row is made up of 16 or 14 beads but the placement of each row—some decreasing at the beginning of the row, some increasing at the end of the row—is what determines the shape and pattern. The rows use a combination of brick stitch and ladder stitch.

Types of Increases and Decreases

There are three types of increases or decreases. Each will have a label that's used in the row-by-row instructions.

Type 1 is a decrease at the beginning of the row. With the thread exiting the third bead in the previous row, pick up two beads and, skipping a connecting thread, pass under the next connecting thread as shown in figure 1.

Type 2 is an increase at the beginning of the row. With the thread exiting the first bead in the previous row, pick up two beads and pass under the first connecting thread and up through the second bead of the pair. Pass down through the first bead and ladder stitch two beads to extend the row (figure 2). Weave back to the point of origin and continue the row.

Type 3 is an increase at the end of the row. With the thread exiting the last bead in the current row, pick up one bead (figure 3, bead 15) and pass up through the last bead again. Pass down through the last bead added (bead 15), and pick up one bead (bead 16). Pass back down through bead 15 and up through the last bead before the increase.

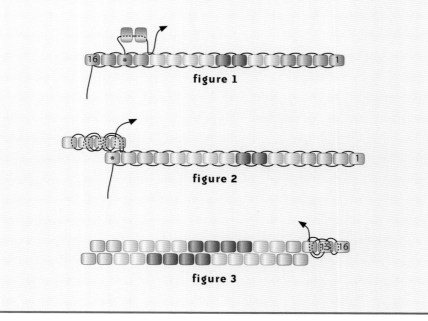

figure 1

figure 2

figure 3

► Flame Design

Row 1 Make a bead ladder following the color pattern in figure 4, beginning at the point shown with the red star. After adding 16 beads, weave back to bead 14.

Row 2 With A, work a Type 1 decrease (see Overview at left). Continue with brick stitch and add two As, two Cs, four Bs, and four As. Work a Type 3 increase (see Overview) with A.

Follow the colors charted in figure 5 for rows 3 through 11.

Row 3 This is a 14-bead row of regular brick stitch. Pick up two As and pass under the first connecting thread in the row.

Row 4 Pick up two As and pass under the second connecting thread. Follow the color pattern to add 11 more beads. Add the final bead of the row with a diagonal brick stitch increase.

Row 5 Begin with a Type 2 increase (see Overview). Pick up two As and pass under the first connecting thread and then up through the second bead of the pair. Pass down through the first bead and add two beads with ladder stitch. Weave back to the point of origin, and continue the row, following the color chart.

Row 6 This is the center row of the piece. Begin with a Type 1 decrease in color A. Work regular brick stitch following the chart to add 11 more beads. Add one bead with a diagonal brick stitch increase, then add two more beads with ladder stitch.

Row 7 Repeat row 6, following the color chart for row 7.

Row 8 Follow the color chart and work a regular row of diagonal brick stitch.

Row 9 Work a regular row beginning with two As and passing under the second connecting thread.

Row 10 Begin with a Type 2 increase with A and follow the color chart to complete the row.

Row 11 Begin with a Type 1 decrease with A and follow the color pattern to complete the row.

▶ Complete the Earring

1 Using As, bezel the coin pearl with circular peyote stitch, working the final row with 15°s.

2 Attach the bezeled pearl to the inside of the piece as shown in figure 6, then

backstitch a row of 15° charlottes along each side of the piece (the beads outlined in red).

3 With the thread exiting the bottom bead, pick up one B, three 15°s, one drop, three 15°s, and one B. Pass back through the bottom bead. Repeat the thread path to reinforce.

4 Find the center bead at the top of the bezel. With the thread exiting the next bead to the right or left in the same row, pick up one 15°, one A, and one B; pass through the lower loop of the earring wire; pick up one B, one A, and one 15°; pass through the next bead in the same row of the bezel. Reinforce the thread path.

figure 4

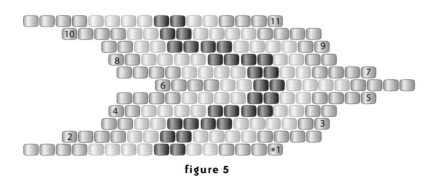

figure 5

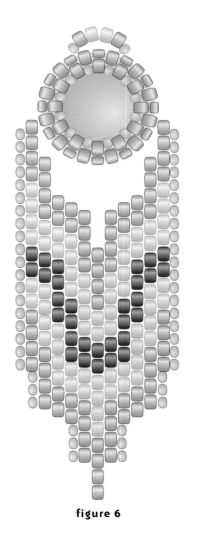

figure 6

SAPPHO NECKLACE

Sappho was a Greek poet whose work rivaled her male colleagues of the sixth and seventh centuries BCE. From the eighteenth century onward, she has often been shown in paintings with a lyre to represent poetic creativity. This soft and elegant necklace has three lyre-shaped components and a unique toggle closure.

► Lyre Components

You'll need three lyre components, which are made with circular peyote stitch, circular brick stitch, and diagonal brick stitch, as follows:

Coin Pearl Bezel

1 Use cylinder beads to bezel a coin pearl with circular peyote stitch. Work a final row with 15° As. This helps secure the pearl and adds contrast.

Repeat to bezel all 16 coin pearls.

Brick Stitch Flange

Refer to figure 1 for rows 1 through 3.

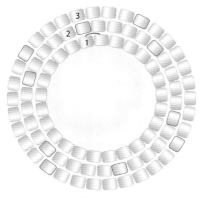

figure 1

Row 1 Here you'll switch from peyote to brick stitch, continuing with cylinder beads. With the thread exiting a bead in row 8 on the outer edge of the bezel, pick up two beads and catch a thread between the two beads next to the exited bead. Pull the thread so the beads lie side by side, with the holes facing up and down. Pass through the second bead of the set. *Pick up one bead, catch a thread between the next two beads in the peyote base, and pass back through the bead. It's important that the beads not be too far apart—try to seat them as close as possible to each other. Repeat from * until the pearl is completely surrounded by a row of brick stitch. With the thread exiting the last bead in the row, close the circle by passing through the first bead in the row, then back through the last bead in the row. You will use approximately 25 beads, depending on the size of the pearl.

Row 2 There will be approximately 30 beads in this row; if necessary, add more to prevent too many open spaces. Pick up two beads and pass under the next connecting thread in the row and up through the second bead in the set. *Pick up one bead and pass under the next connecting thread and up through the bead. Repeat from * and make approximately six increases in the row. The increases are outlined in red in figure 1. When increasing in brick stitch, two beads share a connecting thread but they're added one bead at a time. At the end of the row, join the last bead to the first as you did in row 1.

Row 3 You'll use approximately 34 beads in this row; again, add more beads if necessary to prevent too many open spaces. Work as for row 2, making approximately four increases in the row. The increased beads are outlined in red in figure 1. At the end of the row, join the last bead to the first as you did in row 1. Set the pearl aside.

Repeat rows 1 through 3 to make 11 more bezeled pearls.

Brick Stitch Strips

The four coin pearls used in each lyre shape are joined with three strips of brick stitch—two strips of diagonal brick stitch and one strip of regular brick stitch with a slight curve.

Diagonal Strips

1 Make a bead ladder of 12 cylinder beads.

2 Complete five rows of diagonal brick stitch as shown in figure 2.

Repeat steps 1 and 2 to make five more diagonal strips.

Curved Strip

1 Make a bead ladder of 16 beads to begin the strip.

2 Work a row of regular flat brick stitch, increasing two beads in the middle of the row, as outlined in red in figure 3. To make the increases, work two beads (one at a time) in the connecting thread between the eighth and ninth beads and the ninth and tenth beads of row 1. The increase gives the piece a slight curve.

3 Work three rows of brick stitch without increases.

Repeat steps 1 through 3 to make two more strips.

Join the Components

1 Position the diagonal strip between two bezeled and flanged pearls as shown in figure 4.

2 Refer to figure 5 for joining. With the thread exiting bead 1 of the strip, pass

figure 2

figure 3

figure 4

through bead 1 of the flange. Pass through bead 2 of the flange, then through bead 2 of the strip. Pass through bead 3 of the flange, then through bead 4 of the flange, then through bead 4 of the strip. Complete the join by passing through bead 5 of the flange.

3 Repeat step 2 on the other end of the strip.

4 Repeat steps 1 through 3 to make five more components.

Refer to figure 6 for steps 5 through 8.

5 Line up two components as shown and join them by stitching into beads in both flanges.

6 Position a curved strip as shown so that the bottom pearls fan out. Attach the top rows to the diagonal strip and the bottom three rows to the flange. Tack the strip securely by passing through a bead in the diagonal strip and then through a bead in the curved strip or the flange.

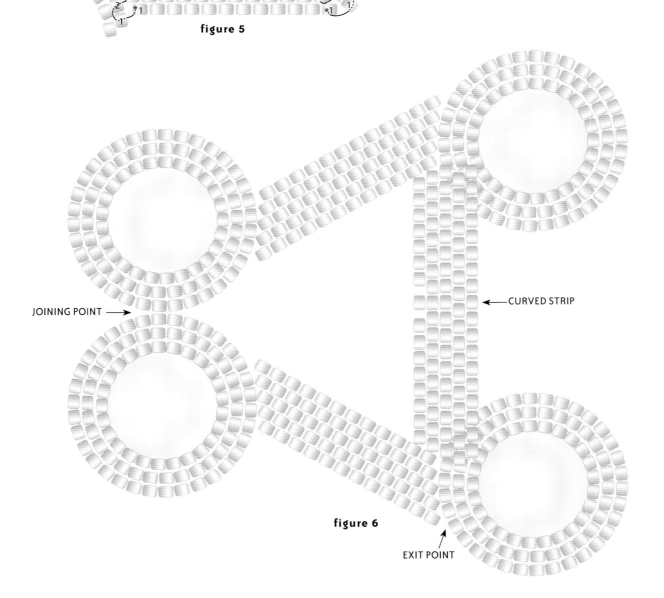

figure 5

figure 6

JOINING POINT →

CURVED STRIP

EXIT POINT

7 Repeat steps 5 and 6 to create two more lyre shapes.

8 To finish the lyres, backstitch around all edges of each piece, beginning at the exit point shown in the following pattern: one 15° B, one 15° A, one 2-mm crystal, one 15° A, and one 15° B.

9 Join the top flanges of the three lyres with ladder stitch through three beads used in the backstitch edging.

▶ Chain

The chain is made with varying lengths of single and doubled St. Petersburg chain of squares, 15° A beads, and glass pearls. The instructions follow; you'll need six doubled chains and two single chains in the following lengths:

- 2 doubled chains, each 2½ inches (6.4 cm) long
- 2 doubled chains, each 3 inches (7.6 cm) long
- 2 doubled chains, each 5 inches (12.7 cm) long
- 2 single chains, each 1¼ inches (3.2 cm) long

Refer to figure 7 for steps 1 through 3.

1 String on a stopper bead, pick up six squares, and pass through the third and fourth bead.

2 Pick up one 15° A and pass back down through three squares.

3 Pick up one glass pearl and pass through the fifth and sixth square beads. Continue with St. Petersburg chain to the length required.

4 To double the chain, start a new thread and repeat steps 1 and 2. Pass through the glass pearl on the first chain and through the two squares as shown in figure 8. *Pick up four squares and pass through the first and second beads. Pick up one 15° and pass back through three squares. Pass through the pearl and two squares. Continue from * until the chain is completed (figure 9).

5 Notice that one end of the chain is wider than the other end. The narrow end is the one that has the stopper beads. To make this end of the chain ready to attach, ladder stitch together the two beads outlined in red in figure 9.

figure 7

figure 8

figure 9

▶ Closure

The necklace closes with a toggle bar made of two of the remaining bezeled pearls and a small strip of diagonal brick stitch. The bar fits through a loop made of single St. Petersburg chain.

1 Make a bead ladder of seven cylinder beads and work two rows of diagonal brick stitch.

2 Attach one end of the strip to one of the bezeled pearls and repeat on the other end of the strip (figure 10). Embellish by backstitching around the strip and pearls with the same pattern used on the lyre shapes.

3 To make the loop, make a small strip (approximately 2 inches [5.1 cm] long) of single St. Petersburg chain, following the pattern in figure 7. **Note:** Adjust the length as needed depending on the size of the toggle.

4 Fold the loop in half and ladder stitch the squares on either end of the strip together to form a loop.

▶ Assemble

1 Attach the wider end of a 2½-inch (6.4 cm) length of chain to the side edging of the top pearl on one side of the lyre.

2 Attach the wider end of a 3-inch (7.6 cm) length of chain to the side edging of the bottom pearl of the lyre.

3 Join the narrow ends of the two chains together by making a single right angle weave unit as follows: With the thread exiting the inner end set of square beads on one piece of the chain, pick up one glass pearl and pass down through the corresponding set of square beads on the other piece of the chain. Pick up one glass pearl and pass through the first set of

squares to complete the right angle weave unit (figure 11).

4 Attach this joined end of chain to one of the remaining bezeled pearls.

5 Repeat steps 1 through 4 on the other side of the necklace.

6 Attach the single pieces of chain so they span the opening between the chains just attached.

7 Attach the wide end of a 5-inch (12.7 cm) piece of chain to the top of the bezeled pearl added in step 4 and the other end to the loop for the closure. Repeat on the other side, attaching the toggle to this end.

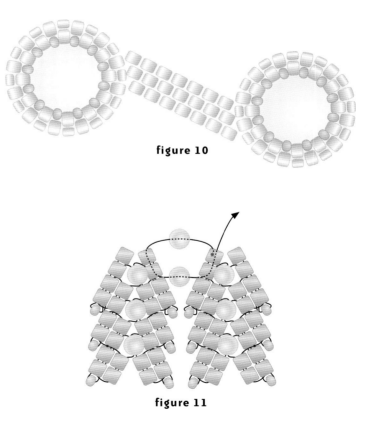

figure 10

figure 11

KILIM BEADS PENDANT

The Kilim Beads Pendant evolved after I made the Anatolia necklace. I was playing with the cross shapes used in that piece, trying to develop a three-dimensional component. When I joined the crosses, it resulted in the frame for a bead. The insert is an Anatolian rug motif that some believe wards off the evil eye.

▶ Frame

Start by creating two cross pieces using cylinder As for the outline beads and cylinder Bs for the inner beads.

1 Pick up four cylinder As and pass through them again to form a circle. Step up through the first bead.

2 Pick up one cylinder A and pass through the next bead in the circle. Repeat to add one bead between each of the beads in row 1. Step up through the first bead added in this row.

3 Pick up two cylinder As and pass through the next bead in row 2. Repeat to add two beads between each of the beads in row 2. Step up through the first bead added in this row, splitting the pair (figure 1, beads 1 and 2). You're now in position to begin one of the arms of the cross.

4 Pick up one cylinder B (figure 2, bead 3) and pass through the next cylinder A (figure 2, bead 2). Pick up one cylinder A (figure 2, bead 4) and pass through the cylinder B just added (figure 2, bead 3).

figure 1

figure 2

SUPPLIES

Basic Beading Kit (page 11)

Size 11° cylinder beads:

   Color A, antiqued gold, 5 g

   Color B, matte brick, 5 g

   Color C, matte pale blue, 2 g

   Color D, matte dark blue, 2 g

1 round semiprecious bead, 4 mm

1 briolette drop, 6 x 9 mm

1 round semiprecious bead, 2 mm

18 inches (45.7 cm) of gemstone and gold chain

1 gold lobster claw clasp, 6 mm

2 gold split rings, 5 mm

Glad Press'n Seal

FINISHED SIZE

Pendant, 3⅞ inches (10 cm) long

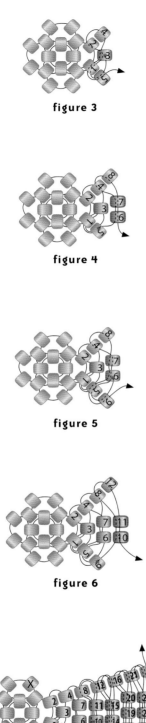

figure 3

figure 4

figure 5

figure 6

5 Make a figure-eight odd-count peyote turn as follows. Pick up one cylinder A (figure 3, bead 5), and pass through beads 1, 3, 2, and 4. Complete the figure eight by passing back through beads 3, 1, and 5. You're in position to add the next set of beads.

6 Pick up two cylinder Bs (figure 4, beads 6 and 7) and pass through the next cylinder A (bead 4). Pick up one cylinder A (figure 4, bead 8) and pass back through beads 7 and 6.

7 Pick up one cylinder A (figure 5, bead 9) and pass through beads 5, 6, 7, 4, and 8. Pass back through beads 7, 6, and 5, and then back through the first bead added, bead 9.

8 With the thread exiting bead 9, pick up two cylinder Bs (figure 6, beads 10 and 11) and pass through bead 8. With the thread exiting bead 8, pick up one cylinder A (bead 12) and pass through beads 11 and 10.

9 Refer to figure 7 for the remaining rows. With the thread exiting bead 10, pick up one cylinder A (bead 13) and pass through beads 9, 10, 11, 8, and 12. To complete the figure-eight turn, pass back through beads 11, 10, and 9, and the first bead added, bead 13.

10 With the thread exiting bead 13, pick up two cylinder Bs (beads 14 and 15) and pass through bead 12. Pick up one cylinder A (bead 16) and pass through beads 15 and 14.

11 With the thread exiting bead 14, pick up one cylinder A (bead 17) and make the figure-eight turn through beads 13, 14, 15, 12, and 16, then back through 15, 14, 13, and 17.

12 Pick up three cylinder Bs (beads 18, 19, and 20) and pass through bead 16. Pick up one cylinder A (bead 21) and pass back through beads 20, 19, and 18.

13 With the thread exiting bead 18, pick up one cylinder A (bead 22) and make the figure-eight turn as before, exiting bead 22. Pick up three cylinder Bs (beads 23, 24, and 25) and pass through bead 21. Pick up one cylinder A (bead 26) and go back through beads 25, 24, and 23.

14 To make the last figure-eight turn for this arm, pick up one cylinder A (bead 27) and make the figure-eight turn to exit the same bead, bead 27. Pick up three cylinder Bs (beads 28, 29, and 30) and pass through bead 26.

15 Weave through to the starting point for the next arm (marked with an X in figure 7) and repeat steps 1 through 14. Complete the remaining two arms for the cross shape. Tie off the thread.

16 Line the pieces up as shown in figure 8. The beads outlined in red on both crosses in the diagram are the beads to be stitched together. Individually square stitch the three inside color beads on one arm to the corresponding three inside color beads on the other arm (figure 9). With the thread

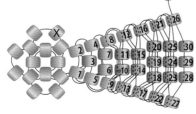

figure 7

exiting an end bead of one of the sets, pick up one cylinder A and pass through the other set of three beads; pick up one cylinder A and pass through the first set of three beads. The added beads sit perpendicular on each side.

17 Weave through the beadwork and repeat step 2 on the remaining three arms.

▶ **Pattern Inserts**

1 With the thread exiting a perpendicular bead added in step 16 above, make an eight-bead ladder of one C, one B, one D, two As, one D, one B, and one C. Join the ladder to the corresponding perpendicular bead.

2 Pass through the next lower set of three inside beads, the perpendicular edge bead, the set of three beads above, and the outline bead above the perpendicular bead, as shown in figure 10.

3 Work a seven-bead row of brick stitch with one C, one B, one D, one A, one D, one B, and one C. At the end of the row,

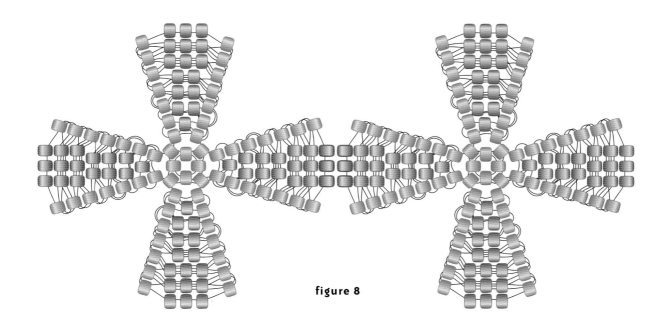

figure 8

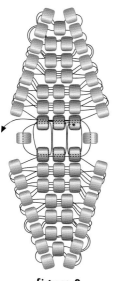

figure 9

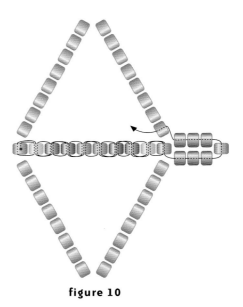

figure 10

pass through the outline bead above the perpendicular bead, turn, and pass through the next outline bead above (figure 11).

4 Work six rows of brick stitch following the color pattern in figure 12, making turns through the outline beads as illustrated.

5 Weave through the beadwork and repeat steps 3 and 4 for the other half of the insert.

Repeat steps 1 through 5 to complete two more brick inserts, alternating the colors in the pattern to give a slightly different look to the next frame.

6 Repeat steps 1 through 4 to complete the first half of the insert. Stuff the component with Press'n Seal, then repeat step 5 to complete this last insert.

Repeat all steps to make three beaded components total.

▶ Join the Components

To join the three beads into a pendant, you'll build off the end with the holes and zip the pieces together.

1 With the thread exiting a bead in row 3 of the cross-shaped frame on one end of the first bead, *pick up two As and pass through the next bead in the row (figure 13). Repeat from * for the entire row, adding a total of four sets of two beads. At the end of the row, step up through the first bead added, splitting the pair.

2 *Pick up one bead and pass through the second bead of the pair; pick up one bead and pass through the first bead of the next pair. Repeat from * for the entire row. Step up through the first bead added.

3 Next, complete two rows of regular peyote stitch.

4 Repeat steps 1 through 3 on the second bead and work one additional row of peyote stitch.

5 Zip the two beads together.

Repeat steps 1 through 5 to join the third bead to the second bead.

▶ Add the Drop

1 With the thread exiting a bead in row 3 at the center portion of the bottom bead, pick up three As, the 4-mm bead, three As, the drop, and three As.

2 Pass back through the 4-mm bead, pick up three As, and pass through the bead in row 3 opposite the original bead exited.

3 Repeat the thread path for additional strength.

▶ Bail

I learned to make triangles in *Diane Fitzgerald's Shaped Beadwork* and I just love using them to make bails. Make a bail of two triangle peyote pieces zipped together with right angle weave as follows:

Row 1 String three beads and tie the thread to form a circle. Step up through the first bead.

Row 2 *Pick up two beads and pass through the next bead in row 1. Repeat from * two more times. Step up through the first bead added, splitting the pair.

Row 3 *Pick up two beads and pass through the second bead of the pair. Pick up one bead and pass through the first bead of the next pair. Repeat from * two more times. Step up through the first bead added, splitting the pair.

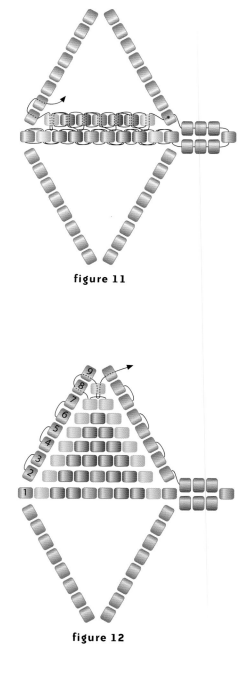

figure 11

figure 12

Row 4 *Pick up two beads and pass through the second bead of the pair; pick up one bead and pass through the next bead; pick up one bead and pass through the first bead of the next pair. Repeat from * two more times. Step up through the first bead added, splitting the pair.

Rows 5–7 Work three more rows as for row 4, adding two beads in the corners and working regular peyote stitch along the sides (figure 14).

Repeat rows 1 through 7 to create another triangle. Add a picot of one A, one 2-mm bead, and one A to the center of the triangle.

With the thread exiting the first up bead on one side of a triangle, work two rows of right angle weave using the up beads as the base beads for each unit. Use a right angle weave zip to join this triangle to the other.

Attach the bail to the center top of the pendant by stitching the two end beads of the tips to beads on the pendant.

► **Assemble**

Attach the lobster clasp to the split ring and then to one end of the gemstone chain. Attach the remaining split ring to the other end of the chain. Run the chain through the bail.

figure 13

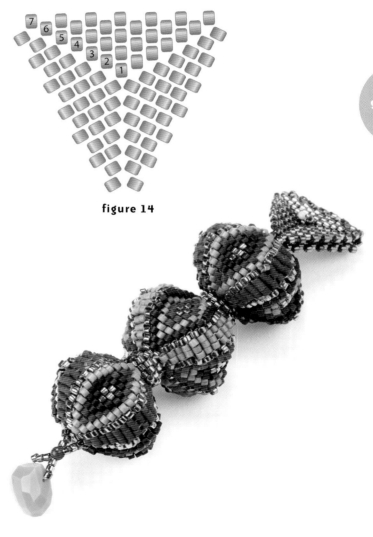

figure 14

CHAPTER FIVE
ARCHITECTURAL ELEMENTS AS INSPIRATION

Architecture and frescoes are challenging to translate into jewelry. Because seed beads are the only medium I work with, I encapsulate the spirit of a design, rather than replicate it exactly. For example, the Gaudí Bead captures the essence of the famed architect's incredible structures by using layers of right angle weave and bright colors, and the Oplonti bracelet references the floral motifs and columns painted in ancient frescoes.

SANTA SOFIA PENDANT

The onion dome church steeples found throughout Italy and Eastern Europe serve as the inspiration for this necklace. I find their shapes very appealing, and I love the colors and patterns found on some of them.

SUPPLIES

Basic Beading Kit (page 11)

Size 11° cylinder beads:

Color A, metallic green iris, 10 g

Color B, topaz luster, 4 g

Size 11° round seed beads, green metallic, 20 g

Size 15° round seed beads, Color B, topaz luster, 1–2 g

4 vitrail Swarovski crystal drops (5500 series), 6 x 9 mm

Faceted crystal rondelles, 3 mm:

Emerald, 10

Topaz, 23–27

5 faceted Swarovski rondelles, topaz, 6 mm

1 freshwater pearl drop, 6 x 9 mm

1 coin pearl, 10 mm

Fireline or Wildfire, size .006

FINISHED SIZE

Pendant, 3 inches (7.6 cm) long

Chain, 22 inches (55.9 cm) long

Figure 1 shows the completion of steps 1 through 6.

1 Using cylinder A and B beads, make a circular peyote stitch disc following the color pattern shown in figure 1.

Row 1 Pick up three beads and pass through the beads again to form a circle. Step up at the end of the row by passing through the first bead again.

Row 2 *Pick up one bead and pass through the next bead in row 1. Repeat from * two more times, then step up through the first bead added.

Row 3 Here's where the increase begins. *Pick up two beads and pass the needle through the next bead in row 2. Repeat from * two more times to complete the

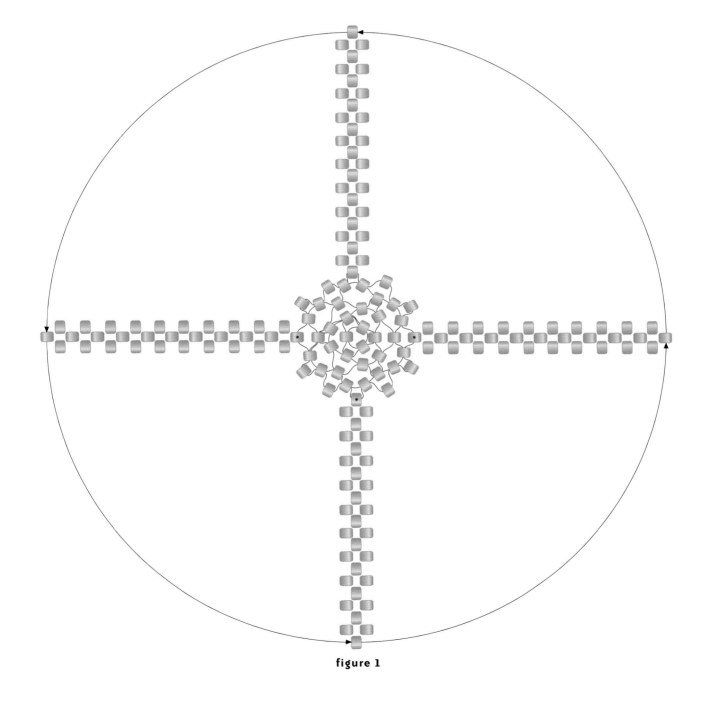

figure 1

row, adding a total of six beads. At the end of the row, step up through the first bead added, splitting the pair (figure 2).

Row 4 Here's the second step of the gradual increase. With the thread exiting the first bead in a pair, *pick up one bead and pass through the second bead of the pair. Pick up one bead and pass through the first bead of the next pair added in row 3.

Repeat from * for the entire row, adding a total of six beads. At the end of the row, step up through the first bead added in this row (figure 3).

Row 5 Work as for row 3, adding a total of 12 beads. At the end of the row, step up through the first bead added, splitting the pair.

Row 6 Work as for row 4, adding a total of 12 beads (figure 4).

2 Pick up four beads and pass through the same bead exited from the opposite end to create a right angle weave unit.

3 Make a base row of 10 right angle weave units, creating the first spine for the armature. Weave back down the row to strengthen the spine and return to the circular peyote core.

4 Weave through six beads in the core (three up beads and three down beads) and create another spine of 10 right angle weave units. Weave back to the core of the piece as done in step 3.

5 Repeat step 4 to complete two more spines for a total of four spines. **_Note:_** When weaving the fourth spine, weave through each unit twice and end with the thread exiting the top of the unit. You need to weave through the units twice to match the tension of the other spines.

6 With the thread exiting the top bead of the last right angle weave unit, pass through the top beads of the next three right angle weave units, being careful not to twist the spines. Pull the spines together to form the armature. Reinforce by passing through the four top beads again.

7 With the thread exiting an end bead, pick up one cylinder B and pass through the next bead. Repeat three more times, adding one cylinder B between the four end beads (figure 5).

figure 2

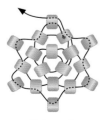

figure 3

figure 4

figure 5

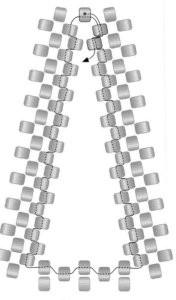

figure 6

▶ Dome

The side beads of the right angle weave spines become the up beads for working a variation of tubular peyote stitch in each quadrant using cylinder A beads. The right angle weave up beads are considered row 1.

Row 2 Refer to figure 6 for all steps of this row. Pass through one of the side beads of a right angle weave unit, pick up one cylinder B, and pass through the next up bead. The end bead exited, the first bead passed through, and the new bead picked up are referred to as the "trio" in each quadrant and are outlined in red in the illustration.

*Pick up a bead and pass through the next up bead. Repeat from * to add eight more beads down the side of the quadrant, three beads along the base, and nine beads up the other side for a total of 21 beads in this row. Step up through the trio, exiting the first bead added.

Row 3 Work a peyote stitch row with 20 beads. **Tip:** It helps to count the beads for each row ahead of time. The 20 beads added in this row are outlined in red in figure 7. After adding the last of the 20 beads, pass through the first bead added in row 1, and step up through the first bead added in this row. This step up/decrease is done at the end of every row of each quadrant.

Row 4 Work a row of 19 beads. Notice how the base of the dome increases—this is the space where you'll add the crystal in row 10.

Rows 5–9 Work peyote stitch with one fewer bead in each row, ending with a 14-bead row.

Row 10 Work a row of 13 beads. Step up as done previously, and add a crystal drop with a figure-eight anchor, passing through the crystal, the center bead on the base of the dome, back up through the crystal, and through the last bead added in the row (figure 8). Step up again through the first bead added in the row.

Row 11 Notice how the crystal wants to sink into the dome. To pull the crystal out of the dome, work one peyote stitch row with 15°s, step up at the end of the row, and anchor the crystal—as done in row 10—to the top and bottom 15°s just added.

You've just finished one of four quadrants. Weave to the same starting point in the next quadrant, then repeat rows 1 through 11 three more times to complete the remaining quadrants.

Bottom of the Dome

Build the bottom of the dome with tubular peyote stitch using cylinder Bs, as follows:

Row 1 With the thread exiting a bead in row 4 of the circular peyote disc (figure 9), pick up two cylinder Bs and pass through the next bead in row 4. Continue adding sets of two beads between the beads in row 4 for a total of six sets of two beads. Step up through the first two beads added.

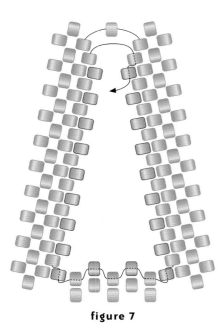

figure 7

figure 8

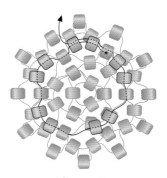

figure 9

I made these earrings using a variation on the instructions given here.

Row 2 *Pick up one bead and pass through the next set of two beads. Repeat from * to complete the row and step up through the first bead added.

Row 3 *Pick up two beads and pass through the next bead. Repeat from * to complete the row and step up through the first bead added, splitting the pair.

Row 4 *Pick up one bead and pass through the second bead of the pair. Pick up one bead and pass through the first bead of the next pair. Repeat from * to complete the row and step up through the first bead added.

Row 5 Complete a row of regular peyote.

Rows 6–13 Repeat rows 1 and 2 until 13 rows have been completed.

Row 14 Complete a row of regular peyote with one bead in each spot. One bead will lie over the two beads in row 12. Step up through the first bead added.

Row 15 *Pick up a bead and pass through the next up bead. Decrease in the next spot by passing through the next up bead without adding a bead. Repeat from * to complete the row. Step up through the first bead added.

Row 16 *Pick up two beads and pass through the next up bead. Repeat from * to complete the row and step up through the first two beads added.

Row 17 *Pick up one bead and pass through the next two beads. Repeat from * to complete the row and step up through the first bead added.

Row 18 Complete a row of regular peyote with one bead in each spot. One bead will lie over two beads in row 17.

Row 19 Repeat row 15.

Row 20 Place one bead in each decrease spot. Pass through the four beads added in this row. Knot and tie off.

Top of the Dome

Row 1 With the thread exiting one of the beads added after the four spines were joined (see figure 2 and step 7 of the Base), pick up two cylinder Bs and pass through the next bead added in step 7. Continue adding two beads between the spines for a total of four sets of two beads (eight

beads total). Step up through the first bead added, splitting the pair.

Row 2 Repeat row 4 of Bottom of the Dome.

Rows 3–7 Work regular peyote without any increases or decreases.

Rows 8–11 Repeat rows 15 through 18 of Bottom of the Dome. Pass through the four beads added in this row. Knot and tie off.

▶ Bail

The bail is made using odd-count flat peyote stitch with decreases on each end.

1 String on a stopper bead and pick up 11° cylinder As. Complete 25 rows of flat peyote stitch.

2 Decrease to a point on each end by catching a thread and making a U-turn back into the beads as shown in figure 10. Repeat on the other end of the bail.

3 Fold the bale and center the tips at the top of the dome. Attach it to the top of the dome component by passing through a bead on one side of the bail tip, a bead at the top of the cone, and then through the bead on the other side of the bail tip. Repeat on the other side of the bail and pass through all beads again until the piece is attached securely.

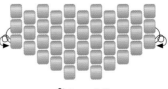

figure 10

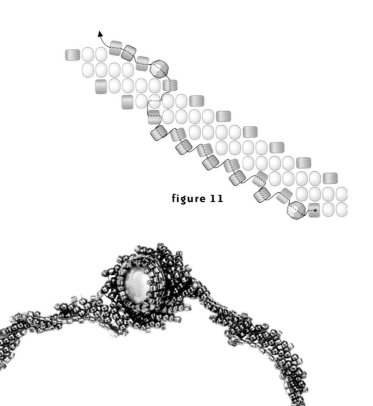

► Embellish

Add embellishment beads to the top of the component, between the quadrants, and to the bottom section as follows:

On Top of the Component

With the thread exiting a set of two beads added in row 1 of Top of the Dome, pick up one 15° round, one emerald rondelle, and one 15° round, and pass through the next set of two. Repeat to add a total of four sets of three beads.

Between the Quadrants

Notice the gaps where the dome section meets the bottom section. Embellishment is definitely needed here! With the thread exiting the base of one of the quadrants, pick up one 15° round, one 6-mm rondelle, and one 15° round, and pass through a corresponding bead in the next quadrant. The crystal embellishment should sit toward the lower part of the quadrant. Repeat to embellish all four quadrants.

On the Base

Add embellishment to the decrease spots in row 15 of the base. With the thread exiting a bead in row 15, pick up one 15° round, one 3-mm emerald rondelle, and one 15° round, and pass through the next bead in row 15. Repeat to add a total of six embellishments.

With the thread exiting one of the four beads at the bottom of the base, pick up three cylinder As, the pearl drop, and one cylinder A; pass back through the pearl and the third cylinder A added; pick up two cylinder As and pass through the corresponding bead in the base. Reinforce.

► Chain

Make a length of St. Petersburg chain 40 to 44 inches (101.6 to 111.8 cm) long, using cylinder Bs for the edges and 11° rounds for the inner section. When you curve the chain in the next step, it will draw in half the length, causing the resulting chain to measure 20 to 22 inches (50.9 to 55.9 cm) long.

Curve the Chain

1 With the thread exiting a cylinder bead on the edge at one end of the chain, pick up one topaz crystal and pass through the next cylinder bead.

2 *Pick up one cylinder bead and pass through the next cylinder bead. Repeat from * four more times.

3 Pass through the 11° rounds and the cylinder bead on the other side as shown in figure 11. Repeat steps 1 and 2.

Repeat steps 1 through 3 for the length of the chain.

► Toggle Closure

1 Using cylinder As, bezel the coin pearl. Attach the bezel to one end of the chain with ladder stitch, passing through beads in the center back of the bezel and 11° rounds on the chain.

2 Wrap the other end of the chain around the bezeled pearl to determine the size needed for the loop. Attach the end of the chain to the determined point to form the loop.

figure 11

ARTEMISIA
EARRINGS

The magnificent knot patterns in the marble floors of Santa Maria Maggiore in Rome provide the inspiration for these earrings. This type of geometric mosaic inlay is attributed to the Cosmati family from twelfth-century Rome. Right angle weave circles join to form a three-dimensional component.

SUPPLIES

Basic Beading Kit (page 11)

Size 15° round seed beads:

    Color A, shiny metallic gold, 5 g

    Color B, matte amethyst, 3 g

    Color C, shiny metallic garnet, 3 g

    Color D, mix of metallic and matte medium blue, 3 g

    Color E, matte metallic gold, 1 g

Size 11° cylinder beads, matte metallic gold, < 1 g

2 round garnets, 4 mm

2 pear-shaped freshwater pearl drops with vertical holes, 10 x 15 mm

2 earring posts with 10-mm pads

2 ear nuts

FINISHED SIZE

3⅛ inches (7.9 cm) long

▶ Rings

The rings are stitched with right angle weave in colors B, C, and D, and outlined in color A. Each ring is made in two halves, which are then zipped together.

First Ring

1 Begin by making a strip of right angle weave seven units wide by 19 units long using A and B, and following the pattern in figure 1.

2 Fold the piece in half widthwise and ladder stitch the matching beads on the long ends together.

3 Once the long open end has been closed, pass through the ladder-stitched beads along one edge as shown in figure 2, and then pass through the beads along the other edge to create a curve. This is the first half of one ring.

4 Repeat steps 1 through 3 to complete the second half of the first ring.

5 To complete the ring, zip both sides of the two halves together following the color pattern.

Note: I'm often asked why I don't make one complete circle or other component in structural right angle weave. It's just easier to control tension when working with smaller pieces.

Second and Third Rings

As noted in step 2 below, it's important to tack the three circles together in their interlaced configuration before putting the piece down.

1 Follow steps 1 through 4 for the First Ring, but use C for the inside color. Zip one end of the ring halves together but leave one end open so that it can be connected to the first ring. Place the open end of the second ring over the first ring as shown in figure 3 and zip the remaining end of the ring closed. The two rings are now joined.

2 Follow steps 1 through 4 under First Ring, using D for the inside color, and zip one end of the ring halves together. Place the two joined rings flat on the work surface and interlace the third ring as shown in figure 4. *Don't let go of the piece!* Hold the work firmly and zip the open end of the third ring together.

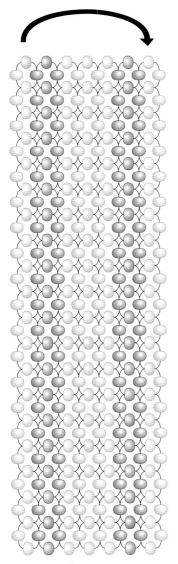

figure 1

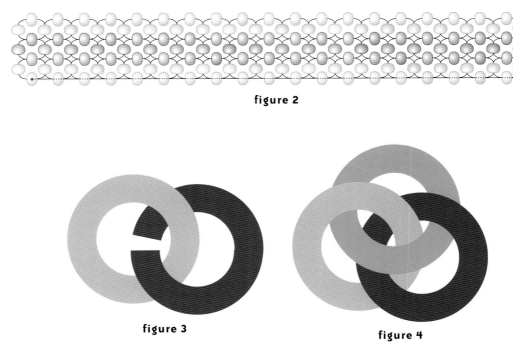

figure 2

figure 3

figure 4

▶ Secure the Rings

If it's possible to pass the needle through beads on the ring to join, do so. If this isn't possible, catch threads between the beads until the three circles are firmly attached to each other at all overlapping points.

▶ Embellish

To give the component definition, use 15° Es to stitch in the right angle weave ditch along the outer edges on both sides of the component.

▶ Earring Post

The post with the 10-mm pad is "captured" with circular peyote as follows.

Rows 1–6 Using size 11° cylinder beads, make a circular peyote piece of six rows.

Rows 7 and 8 Work regular peyote without increases, stepping up at the end of each row. Notice how the piece begins to form a cup and wrap around the back of the 10-mm pad (figure 5).

Row 9 This is a decrease row. *Pick up one bead and pass through the next bead in row 8. To make a gradual decrease, pass

through the next bead in row 7, then the next bead in row 8. Repeat from * around, stepping up through the first bead added in this row. Place the post with the pad face down into the cup and hold it securely.

Row 10 *Pick up two beads and pass through the next bead in row 9. Repeat from * around. Step up through three beads at the end of the row (the last bead of row 9 and the first two added in this row).

Row 11 *Pick up one bead and pass through the next two beads added in row 10. Repeat from * around. Step up through three beads at the end of the row (the last two beads of the previous row and the first bead added in this row).

Row 12 Work regular peyote with no increases or decreases and the beadwork should hold the pad securely. If necessary, complete one more regular row.

▶ Embellish

Embellish the post with a garnet in the center encircled with 15° As, and add three rows of three-bead picots as follows, referring to figure 6 for all steps.

1 Anchor the garnet in the center of the beadwork using a figure-eight anchor.

2 Following the layout in figure 6, add 15° As around the garnet by stitching in the ditch.

3 With the thread exiting a bead in row 4, *pick up three Ds and pass through the next bead in row 4. Repeat from * five more times to complete the row.

4 With the thread exiting a bead in row 5, *pick up one E, one B, and one E; pass through the next bead in row 5. Repeat from * 11 more times to complete the row.

Note: You will be splitting the pairs of beads that were added in row 5, passing through them individually, and adding embellishment beads between.

5 With the thread exiting a bead in row 6, work as for row 5, replacing B with C.

▶ Final Touches

1 Attach the post to the ring component by ladder stitching three beads on the edge of the post to three beads on the top edge of the third circle.

2 Add a drop to the bottom where the two circles meet. Pass through an edge bead on the first circle, pick up two As, one B, two As, the drop, and one A. Pass back through the drop and one A. Pick up one A, one B, and two As. Pass through the corresponding bead of the second circle. Repeat the thread path and secure.

Follow all of the steps above to make the other earring. You may either make it the same as the first earring or switch the position of the bottom two rings for symmetry while wearing, as shown in the sample.

figure 5

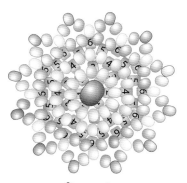

figure 6

GAUDÍ BEAD

One of my favorite artists, the Spanish architect Antonio Gaudí, is world-renowned for his distinct style, which was originally inspired by Gothic architecture. His designs and mosaics are sheer genius, both intricate and surreal. This bead uses both the colors in his mosaics and the shapes in his architecture. It's shown on a Viking Knit chain made by a friend, but it would also look good on a beaded chain of tubular herringbone or peyote stitch.

SUPPLIES

Basic Beading Kit (page 11)

Size 15° round seed beads:

Color A, gold matte metallic, 5 g

Color B, olive green metallic, 2 g

Color C, matte turquoise, 2 g

Color D, purple, 2 g

Color E, gold shiny metallic, 1 g

24 purple Swarovski crystal rounds, 2 mm

12 turquoise Swarovski crystal bi-cones, 3 mm

14 round coral beads, 2 mm

Chain (your choice), 17 inches (43.2 cm) long and approximately 3/16 inch (4 mm) in diameter

1 clasp appropriate for chain

FINISHED SIZE

Bead, 2 inches (5.1 cm) wide x 1 inch (2.5 cm) in diameter

▶ Rings

To make the rings for the Gaudí Bead, you'll use right angle weave with a thread path that allows them to be attached like layers in a wedding cake.

Large Rings

1 Make a strip of right angle weave using size 15° A and B beads following the color pattern in figure 1. The strip is seven units across and 29 units long.

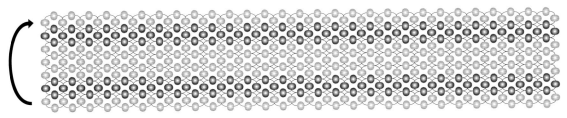

figure 1

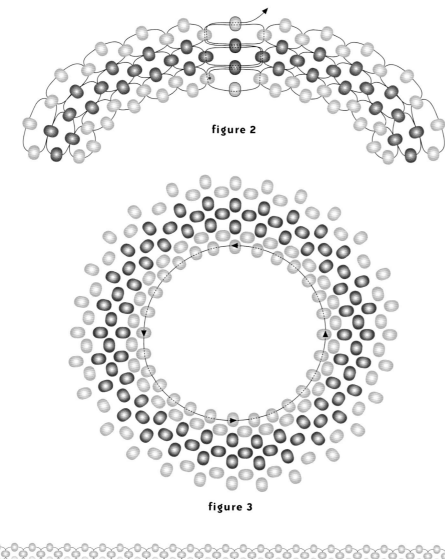

figure 2

figure 3

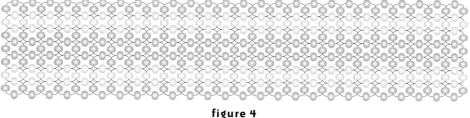

figure 4

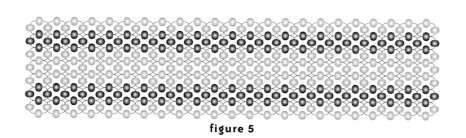

figure 5

2 Fold the piece in half lengthwise and zip up the side with right angle weave, using 15° As.

3 Form the piece into a circle and zip the ends together following the color pattern as shown in figure 2.

4 Shape the circle into a cone by passing through the beads of the inner edge on *one side only* and pulling up taut (figure 3).

Set the ring aside and repeat steps 1 through 4 to make another one.

Medium Rings

Follow steps 1 through 4 for the Large Rings, with the following changes:

• Use C in place of B.

• Make the strip only 26 units long (figure 4).

Set the ring aside and repeat to make another one.

Small Rings

Follow steps 1 through 4 for the Large Rings, but make the following changes:

• Use D in place of B.
• Make the strip 23 units long (figure 5).

Set the ring aside and repeat to make another one.

▶ Make the Bead

Attach the rings by zipping them together with peyote stitch as follows.

1 Position the rings and join them as shown in figure 6. Each half of the bead is made with one large ring, one medium ring, and one small ring, and you'll have to skip three beads on the large ring while joining it to the medium ring and three beads on the medium ring while joining it to the small ring.

2 Position the two halves as shown in figure 7 and zip them together with peyote stitch.

▶ Embellish

Now you'll embellish the bead where the rings were joined with size 15°s, crystals, and coral beads. See figure 8 for placement.

1 *With the thread exiting a bead in the join between the small and medium ring, pick up one E, one crystal round, one E, one crystal bicone, one E, one crystal round, and one E. Place the beads along the join and pass through a bead on the join. Repeat from * for the entire join, and then repeat again on the other end of the bead.

2 With the thread exiting a bead in the join between the medium and large ring, pick up one E, one coral bead, and one E, and pass through the next bead in the join. *Pick up one E and pass through the next bead in the join. Repeat from * for two more beads, then repeat the entire step five more times to add a total of six picots. Repeat on the other end of bead.

3 With the thread exiting a bead in the center where the large rings meet, *pick up three Cs and pass through the next bead in the join; pick up one E and pass through the next bead; pick up three Ds and pass through the next bead in the join; pick up one E and pass through the next bead in the join. Repeat from * around the join.

4 Add Es in the right angle weave ditches on the rows next to the join, between the small and medium rings and the large rings.

▶ Finish

String the bead onto the chain of your choice and add an appropriate clasp if necessary.

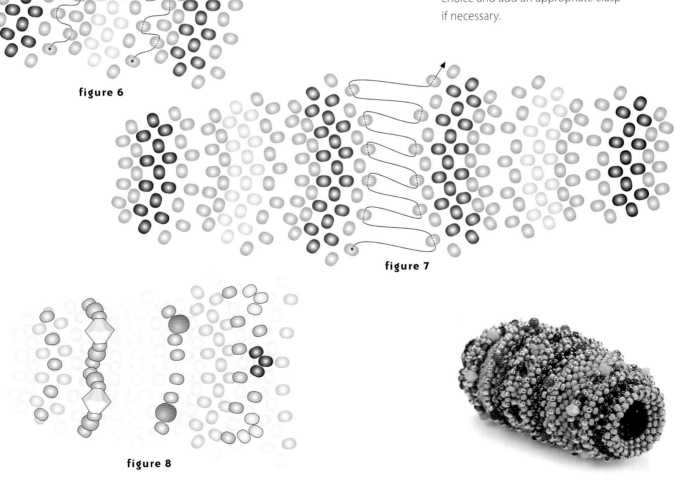

figure 6

figure 7

figure 8

OPLONTI

Villa Oplonti in Naples, a magnificent place that was home to Nero's wife, has got to be my favorite archaeological site. The breathtaking frescoes found near the swimming pool inspired this bracelet. The piece is embellished with vines, ivy leaves, and small "buds" of semiprecious stones. I used a mixture of bead finishes to create the look of an ancient wall.

SUPPLIES

Basic Beading Kit (page 11)

Size 11° cylinder beads:

   Color A, matte opaque antique beige, 10 g

   Color B, ivory luster, 4 g

   Color C, pale cream opal, silver lined, 3 g

   Color D, light bronze metallic, 5 g

   Color E, matte metallic gold, 3 g

Size 15° cylinder beads, metallic green iris, 4 g

Size 15° round seed beads, dark metallic gold, 3 g

Size 15° charlottes, bright metallic gold, 3 g

Approximately 83 dark blue semiprecious beads, 2 mm

1 gold 3-hole tubular bar clasp

FINISHED SIZE

1⅝ x 7 inches (4.7 x 17.8 cm)

► Band

The band for the bracelet is made using singular and two-bead square stitch. For the main part of the band you'll use a mixture of A, B, and C 11° cylinder beads. To create the mix, pick up mostly color A and mix in one or two of colors B and C at a time. The border is made with D and E cylinder beads.

1 Place a stopper bead at the end of the thread. Pick up one D, one E, and one D, pick up 24 beads of A/B/C mix, then pick up one D, one E, and one D.

2 Work the first square stitch row by adding one D, one E, and one D, then add 12 sets of two A/B/C mix, then add one D, one E, and one D (figure 1).

Repeat row 2 until the band measures 6½ inches (16.5 cm) long. Set the band aside.

► Columns

Each column consists of a peyote stitch tube, a brick stitch border, and a circular peyote stitch top. Make two columns, one for each end of the bracelet, as follows.

Tube

1 Place a stopper bead at the end of the thread and pick up 24 A/B/C mix beads.

2 Work 32 rows of two-drop peyote stitch using the A/B/C mix.

3 Zip the first row to the last row to form a tube.

Border

1 With the thread exiting an end bead on the tube, pick up two cylinder Ds, then pass under the connecting thread and through the second bead added to form the first brick stitch. Continue in tubular brick stitch with D to complete the row.

2 Work a row of tubular brick stitch with cylinder Es.

3 Finish the end of the tube with a final row of tubular brick stitch of cylinder Ds.

Repeat steps 1 through 3 on the other end of the tube.

Tops

Use circular peyote stitch and cylinder Ds to make the column tops, which are then attached to each end of the tubes as follows.

Rows 1–6 Complete rows 1 through 6 of circular peyote stitch using cylinder Ds.

Row 7 Work one row of regular peyote without any increases or decreases. Step up through the first bead added.

Row 8 *Pick up two beads and pass through the next up bead in row 7. Pick up one bead and pass through the next up bead in row 7. Repeat from * for the entire row, adding two beads, then one bead. At the end of the row step up through the first two beads added.

Row 9 *Pick up one bead and pass through the next up bead in row 8. Pick up one bead and pass through the pair of up beads in row 8 (treat two beads as one). Repeat from * for the entire row, picking up one bead and passing through one bead, then picking up one bead and passing through two beads. Step up through the first bead added.

Row 10 This is a decrease row. Pick up one bead and pass through the next up bead in row 9. The bead will lie over a pair of beads, pulling the disc in. Complete the entire row with single beads. Step up through the first bead added.

Row 11 Work regular peyote stitch.

Attach the top of the column to one end of the tube by passing under the connecting threads at the top of the tube and then into the up beads in row 11.

Repeat the above steps to make the other top of the column and attach it to the other end of the tube.

figure 1

▶ Attach the Column to the Band

Zip the column to the band as shown in figure 2. Repeat on the other end of the band with the other column.

▶ Ivy Leaves

1 Using 15° cylinders, make a spine of five right angle weave units.

2 Weave back down to the center unit, shown with beads outlined in red in figure 3. Working from the left bead of the center unit, add an arm of three right angle weave units. Weave back to the center unit.

3 Working from the right bead of the center unit, add another arm of three right angle weave units. *Do not weave back to the center unit.* Notice the exit point shown in figure 3. **Tip:** To keep the tension the same as the center spine and the other arm, pass through each unit twice when stitching.

4 With the thread exiting the end bead of a three-unit side strip, pick up one bead and pass through the next low bead in the right angle weave unit (figure 4).

5 Pick up two beads and pass through the low bead of the next right angle weave unit (unit 2).

6 Pick up one bead and pass through the low bead of unit 1. Weave through the center unit to exit the low bead of unit 1

on the other arm. Repeat the pattern *in reverse* to complete the second arm.

7 Weave through the last unit to exit the top bead.

8 Work peyote stitch along the top of the left arm, adding one bead in each spot for a total of two beads (figure 5).

9 Pass through the side bead of unit 2 of the center spine *without* a bead. This is the seam between the arm and the spine and a decrease begins to pull the leaf together.

10 Continue with peyote up to the top of the spine by adding one bead in each spot for a total of three beads.

11 Catch the thread and pass back through the last two beads exited (figure 5).

12 Peyote stitch two beads down the side of the center spine, pass through the next up bead of the left spine, and peyote stitch one bead on the left spine (outlined in red in figure 6).

13 Add one more bead to the left arm and to the center spine, catch a thread and do a U-turn, then pass through the last two beads added twice to ladder stitch them together.

Repeat steps 8 through 13 on the right side of the leaf.

Repeat to make 12 leaves total.

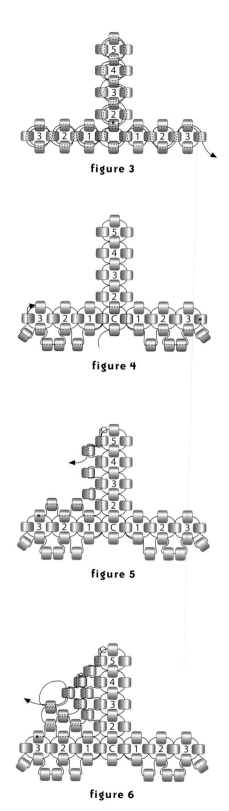

figure 3

figure 4

figure 5

figure 6

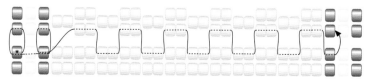

figure 2

▶ Vines

The vines are made with 15° rounds, the ivy leaves, 15° charlottes, and 2-mm semiprecious beads. Switch to a size 13 Sharps needle for working with these smaller beads. See figure 7 for placement.

1 With the thread exiting a bead on the border of the band, pick up seven 15° round beads and attach them to the band either by catching a thread or by bringing the needle through a bead on the band and back into the bead on the vine. To make the vine curve, move the beads into the desired position and tack them down.

2 At the end of the vine, attach one of the ivy leaves and tack it down to the band.

3 Continue with steps 1 and 2 until you've attached seven ivy leaves along the length of the band.

4 With the thread exiting a bead on the border, pick up seven charlottes and tack them down to the band. Pick up three semiprecious stones and pass back into the vine. Continue to add vines of charlottes and clusters of semiprecious stones along both sides of the band.

▶ Closure

1 Center and attach one section of the tube clasp to the underneath section of the column by stitching each hole in the tube to beads on the column. Repeat on the other side.

2 Add vines, leaves, and berries to cover the section between the columns where the clasp shows.

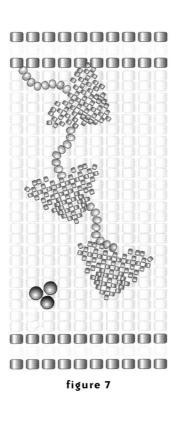

figure 7

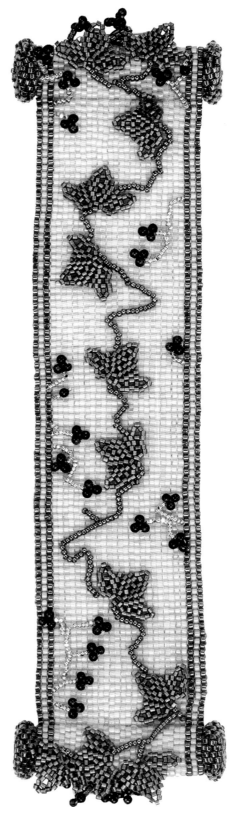

ROSETTE

The rosette motif appears across cultures and is found throughout antiquity in many of the applied arts—jewelry, architecture, and frescoes, for example. There's some evidence that the eight-sided rosette represents birth, death, and rebirth. These rosette earrings replicate the golden ones found in ancient Greek necklaces and funerary crowns.

SUPPLIES

Basic Beading Kit (page 11)

Size 11° matte gold cylinder beads, < 2 g

Size 15° gold metallic round seed beads, < 1 g

2 semiprecious drops, 6 x 9 mm

2 gold ear wires

FINISHED SIZE

1 ⅞ inches (4.7 cm) long

114

► **Front**

Row 1 String four 11° cylinder beads and make a circle of by stepping up through the first bead strung.

Row 2 Work peyote stitch, adding one bead between each of the four beads in row 1. Step up through the first bead added in this row.

Row 3 *Pick up two beads and pass through one bead in row 2 as shown in figure 1. Repeat from * to complete the row. Step up through the first two beads added in this row.

Row 4 *Pick up one bead and pass through two beads (treat two beads as one). Repeat from * to complete the row. Step up through the first bead added in this row (figure 2).

Row 5 *Pick up two beads and pass through one bead as was previously done in row 3. Repeat from * to complete the row. Step up through only the first bead added in this row, splitting the pair (figure 3).

Row 6 *Pick up one bead and pass through the second bead in the pair. Pick up one bead and pass through the first bead in the next pair. Repeat from * to complete the row. Step up through the first bead added in this row (figure 4).

Row 7 *Pick up two beads and pass through one bead in row 6. Repeat from * to complete the row. Step up through the first two beads added in this row.

Row 8 *Pick up one bead and pass through the next pair in row 7. Repeat from * to complete the row. Step up through the first bead added in this row.

Row 9 *Pick up three beads and pass through one bead in row 8. Repeat from * to complete the row. With the front of the rosette complete, you're in position to close the back of the rosette.

► **Back**

Row 1 With the thread exiting a single bead in row 8, *pick up two beads and pass through the next bead in row 8, as shown in figure 5. Repeat from * to complete the row. Step up through the first two beads added in this row.

Rows 1 and 2 are shown in figure 6.

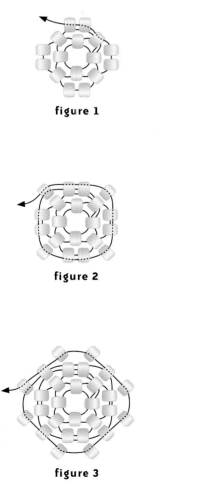

figure 1

figure 2

figure 3

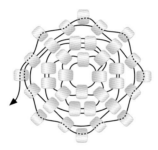

figure 4

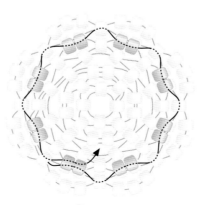

figure 5

figure 6

Row 5 *Pick up one bead and pass through the next up bead, placing one bead in the decrease spot, and weave through to the next decrease spot and repeat. It looks like quite a long distance to travel, but the piece pulls in dramatically and allows the back to remain flat. Repeat from * to complete the row. Pass through the four beads added in this row and tie off the tail thread.

▶ **Embellish and Add the Ear Wire**

Steps 1 through 3 are shown in figure 8.

1 Referring to the illustration for placement, use 15° rounds to stitch in the ditch on the front of the rosette. This gives the rosette definition and the appearance of granulation found in ancient jewelry.

2 With the thread exiting a bead in row 9 of the rosette front, pick up five 15° rounds, one drop, and two 15° rounds. Pass back through the third 15° added, pick up two more 15° rounds, and pass through the next bead in row 9.

3 With the thread exiting a bead in row 9 opposite the drop, add a loop of 15° rounds, pass through the loop on the ear wire, back through the first 15° added, then through the next bead in row 9.

Row 2 *Pick up one bead and pass through two beads in row 1. Repeat from * to complete the row. Step up through the first bead added in this row.

Row 3 *Pick up one bead and pass through one bead in row 2. Repeat from * to complete the row. Step up through the first bead added in this row.

Row 4 This row has a gradual decrease. *Pick up one bead, pass through the next up bead, then pass through the next down bead and the next up bead, decreasing in this spot. Repeat from * to complete the row, decreasing in every other spot. Step up through the first bead added and the first bead passed through in this row (figure 7).

figure 7

figure 8

IL GIARDINO

The *giardini*—the gardens—of ancient Italy, which are often depicted in frescoes on villa walls, were full of lush flowers and foliage. This bangle was inspired by those paintings. It's made of odd-count tubular peyote stitch mounted over a flexible tube and embellished with vines of semiprecious stones.

SUPPLIES

Basic Beading Kit (page 11)

Size 11° cylinder beads:

    Color A, off-white silver-lined, 5 g

    Color B, light bronze, < 1 g

    Color C, matte metallic gold, < 1 g

Size 15° cylinder beads:

    Color B, light bronze, < 1 g

    Color D, green metallic, < 1 g

18 small seed pearls, about the size of 11° seed beads

Approximately 225 round lapis beads, 2 mm

40–50 round pink coral beads, 2 mm

1 silver tube flex bracelet, 8 x ⅛ inch (20.3 cm x 3 mm)

FINISHED SIZE

7 inches (17.8 cm) in circumference

► Tube

String on nine 11° As, pass through them again to form a circle, then pass again through the first bead strung. Continue with peyote stitch by picking up a bead, skipping a bead, and passing through the next bead in the base row (figure 1). **Note:** There's no step up in odd-count tubular peyote; at the end of the row you just keep going. Continue until the tube measures 8 inches (20.3 cm) long.

► End Caps

Make brick stitch bands and peyote stitch caps to attach to the tube as follows:

1 Make a bead ladder of 14 size 11° Bs. Complete one row of brick stitch with 11° Cs, then one more row with 11° Bs (figure 2).

2 Place the band over one end of the tube so that it covers the last three rows. Beginning at one end of the band, join the bottom edge to the tube, following the thread path in figure 3. **Note:** You'll need to wing it a little because you're joining brick to peyote stitch and there are five more beads in the band than in the tube. Just make sure you have a smooth and secure join. When you reach the other end of the band, join the two ends of the band together.

3 Using 11° Bs, complete a "cap" made with five rows of circular peyote, as shown in figure 4.

4 Attach the cap to the open end of the brick stitch band, following the thread path in figure 5.

5 Slide the peyote tube over the flex tube and repeat steps 1 through 4 to close the other end of the bracelet.

6 Embellish the caps by stitching in the ditches of rows 1 and 3 in a pattern of *one 15°, one seed pearl, and one 15°; repeat from * to complete the row(s).

► Vines

1 With the thread exiting a bead near one of the end caps, pick up five 15° Bs and three lapis beads. Pass back through the cylinder beads and attach to the peyote tube. With the thread exiting one of the 15°s on the stem, pick up three 15° Bs and three lapis beads; pass back through the three 15°s beads and attach to the tube (figure 6). Continue making vines with lapis along and around the tube, varying the number of beads in the stems and attaching the stems to the base. Don't be afraid to make the vines lush. Tie off the lapis vine at the other end of the bracelet.

2 Make smaller vines along and around the tube using 15° Ds and the small coral beads.

figure 1

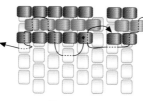

figure 3

figure 2

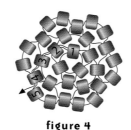

figure 4

GALLERY

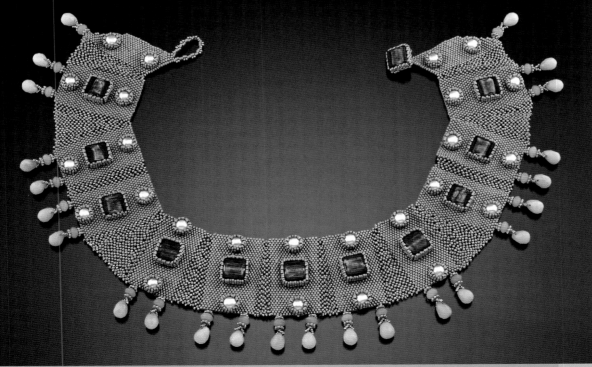

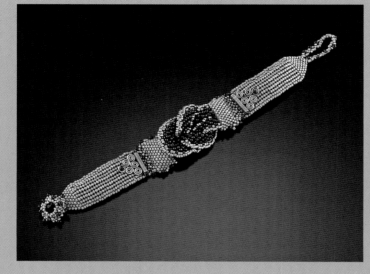

LEFT

Hercules Knot Bracelet, 2004

17.8 x 3.8 x 0.6 cm

Garnets, seed beads, gold vermeil findings, freshwater pearls; right angle weave, herringbone, brick stitch

PHOTO BY LARRY SANDERS

BOTTOM LEFT

Penelope's Crown, 2008

20.3 x 50.8 x 1.9 cm

Hand-carved cameo, seed beads, freshwater pearls; Russian spiral, right angle weave, peyote stitch

PHOTO BY LARRY SANDERS

BOTTOM RIGHT

Bacchus Bracelet, 2008

20.3 x 4.4 x 3.8 cm

Seed beads, drops; right angle weave, peyote stitch

PHOTO BY LARRY SANDERS

Clodia's Necklace, 2008

25.4 x 3.8 x 0.6 cm

Seed beads, opals, gemstones;
right angle weave

PHOTO BY LARRY SANDERS

BOTTOM

Mosaic Chain Cuff, 2006

20.3 x 5.1 x 0.6 cm

Freshwater pearls, seed beads; peyote stitch,
brick stitch

PHOTO BY LARRY SANDERS

LEFT

Santa Sofia Pendant, 2006

10.2 x 3.2 x 2.5 cm

Freshwater pearls, gemstones, seed beads; right angle weave, peyote stitch

PHOTO BY LARRY SANDERS

BOTTOM

Castellani Necklace, 2009

25.4 x 26.7 x 1.3 cm

Carved scarabs, seed beads; square stitch, brick stitch, peyote stitch

PHOTO BY GEORGE POST

TOP

Olivia, **2010**

15.2 x 19.1 x 1.3 cm

Seed beads, freshwater pearls; right angle weave, peyote stitch

PHOTO BY GEORGE POST

CENTER

Iside, **2009**

7.6 x 7 x 2.5 cm

Seed beads, freshwater pearls; peyote stitch, right angle weave

PHOTO BY GEORGE POST

BOTTOM

Toscana, **2010**

5.1 x 11.4 x 1.3 cm

Seed beads, garnets; peyote stitch, right angle weave, Nepal chain

PHOTO BY GEORGE POST

TOP

Pendant & Earrings, 2010

2 x 2.5 x 1.3 cm

Seed beads, freshwater pearls, rubies; peyote stitch

PHOTO BY GEORGE POST

BOTTOM

Pendant 2 & Earrings, 2010

2 x 2.5 x 1.3 cm

Seed beads, freshwater pearls, pyrite; peyote stitch

PHOTO BY GEORGE POST

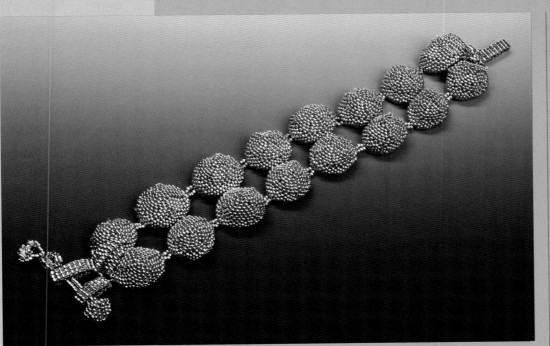

Conchiglie Necklace, 2005

55.9 x 1.9 x 0.3 cm

Cylinder beads,
freshwater pearls

PHOTO BY TOM VAN EYNDE

Pelta Necklace, 2006

81.3 x 30.5 x 0.3 cm

Glass cylinder beads, glass
square beads, sterling
silver beads, semiprecious
stones; right angle weave,
herringbone stitch

PHOTO BY LARRY SANDERS

Armille d'Oro, 2003

17.8 x 4.4 x 1.9 cm

24-karat gold-plated
cylinder beads

PHOTO BY TOM VAN EYNDE

ABOUT THE AUTHOR

PHOTO BY GIULIA CARUNCHIO

Maggie Meister is a designer and an instructor of beaded jewelry whose designs came to fruition when her family moved to Naples in 1998 and her lifelong passions in history, archaeology, and beads merged. In Italy, she was surrounded by sources of inspiration and memories, which she captured with seed beads. She teaches workshops in the United States, Italy, Germany, and Turkey, and her work has been exhibited in Milan and Capri. Maggie's designs have been published in *Masters: Beadweaving* (Lark Crafts, 2008), and in such publications as *Beadwork*, *Bead & Button*, and *RavennAntica*.

Maggie's website is www.amphoradesigns.net. She lives in Norfolk, Virginia, with her husband, Ray, and two sons, Erik and Karl, who have encouraged and supported her endeavors every step of the way.

ACKNOWLEDGMENTS

I could fill a book with the names of everyone who's been part of my realizing my dream. Never in my life did I imagine I would see the world as I have and spend my days doing what I love—designing and teaching beadwork.

First and most important in my life, thanks to my wonderful husband, Ray, and my two sons, Erik and Karl. Ray has supported and encouraged me every step of the way with his advice and love. My boys—who are now men—have helped with very honest opinions and the math! I thank them all for putting up with my crazy travel schedule and absences from home. Thanks to my dad, Irving Martin, for instilling a love of history, archaeology, and, believe it or not, beads! He was always fascinated with the process of beading and used to play with beads as a young boy. Thanks to my mom, Lorraine. We have a mutual love of jewelry, and I still marvel at the contents of her jewelry box and sense of style.

I'm so fortunate to have as a friend and mentor Kathy Dannerbeck and her husband, Peter Dannerbeck. Kathy is truly my sister of the heart.

I'm grateful, too, to Aldo Sparice and his beautiful wife, Angela. His knowledge of his beloved Naples opened my eyes to a whole new world. I love their cooking, as well!

My dear friend Giulia Carunchio guides me and welcomes me into her beautiful home. I cherish our evening chats.

Cheryl Cobern-Browne inspired me to teach with Beadventure Travel when it never even crossed my mind.

My webmaster, Marilyn Langdon, taught me how to send an email and has now created a monster.

Where would any of us be without the wonderful teachers we've studied with? To name a few close to my heart: Carol Wilcox Wells, NanC Meinhardt (who always gives me permission to follow my heart), Jeannette Cook (who joins me on Ireland treks), and Cynthia Rutledge (a national treasure).

To all of my students—your creativity never ceases to amaze me, and being with you is such a blast! Thanks to the gals who helped with the instructions: Lin Behan, Dawn Curtiss, Cheryl Frasca, Lisa Garoon, June Knuth, Debi Larson, and Shelly Kruse. Thanks to all of the shop owners who invited me to teach for them and are now great friends, particularly Carole Tripp, who always lends an ear.

A big huge hug and thanks to technical editor Judith Durant for her patience and fabulous edits. I learned so much. Also to illustrators J'aime Allene and Bonnie Brooks—I wish I had their talent for graphics.

And to Ray Hemachandra and Nathalie Mornu at Lark Crafts: their guidance is priceless.

ADDITIONAL PHOTO CREDITS

Page 23

Top: photo by author

Center: 57.375, *Bracelet from the Olbia Treasure*, Anonymous, Greek, Elements: late 2nd century BC; Setting: 1st century BC; gold, garnet, amethyst, emerald, pearl, chrysoprase, glass, enamel, and modern replacements; 2¹⁄₁₆ x 3⅛ inch (5.3 x 7.9 cm). Photo © The Walters Art Museum, Baltimore.

Bottom left: © iStockphoto.com/petrzurek

Bottom right: © iStockphoto.com/traveller1116

Page 63

Top left: © iStockphoto.com/LanceB

Top right: © iStockphoto.com/imagestock

Bottom left: © iStockphoto.com/onfilm

Bottom right: © Shutterstock/Daniel Gilbey Photography

Page 97

Top left: © Shutterstock/Mi.Ti

Top right: © iStockphoto.com/zensu

Left center: Photo by author

Bottom left: © Shutterstock/Kenneth Sponsler

Bottom right: © iStockphoto.com/GiorgioMagini

BIBLIOGRAPHY

Fitzgerald, Diane. *Diane Fitzgerald's Shaped Beadwork*. Asheville, NC: Lark Crafts, 2009.

Wells, Carol Wilcox. *Creative Bead Weaving*. Asheville, NC: Lark Crafts, 1998.

INDEX

AN ESSENTIAL LIBRARY OF BOOKS FOR BEADERS

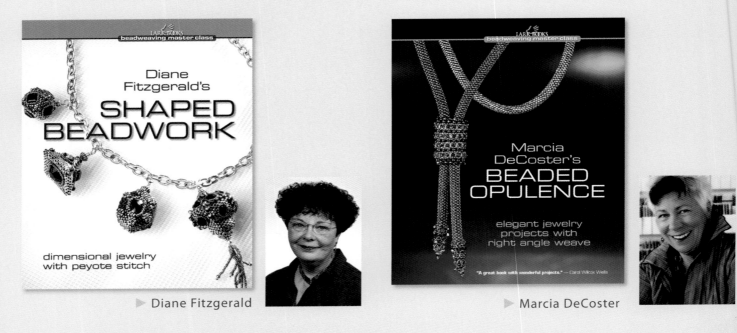

Diane Fitzgerald's
SHAPED BEADWORK

dimensional jewelry with peyote stitch

▶ Diane Fitzgerald

Marcia DeCoster's
BEADED OPULENCE

elegant jewelry projects with right angle weave

"A great book with wonderful projects." — Carol Wilcox Wells

▶ Marcia DeCoster

▶ Laura McCabe

▶ Sherry Serafini

Laura McCabe's
EMBELLISHED BEADWEAVING

jewelry lavished with fringe, fronds, lacework & more

Sherry Serafini's
SENSATIONAL BEAD EMBROIDERY

25 inspiring jewelry projects

"Few, if any, people throughout the course of bead history have taken beads to this thrilling new height." — DIANE FITZGERALD